When

Farmers

Stood Up

When Farmers Stood Up

How the Historic Kisan Struggle in India Unfolded

Ashok Dhawale

FOREWORD BY *Vijay Prashad*

LeftWord

First published by LeftWord Books in April 2022.
Reprinted June 2022

LeftWord Books
2254/2A, Shadi Khampur
New Ranjit Nagar
New Delhi 110008
INDIA

LeftWord Books and Vaam Prakashan are imprints of
Naya Rasta Publishers Pvt. Ltd.

leftword.com

ISBN 978-93-92018-48-0 (paperback)
978-93-92018-53-4 (e-book)

Visit website

If agriculture goes wrong,
nothing else will have a chance to go right.

– M.S. SWAMINATHAN

Chairperson, National Commission on Farmers

Dedicated to the 715 brave martyrs
of the historic farmers' struggle
including the five at Lakhimpur Kheri
who were brutally butchered
by the powers that be

Contents

Foreword:

Thank God for the Farmers

Vijay Prashad

The state of the Indian union is fractured; a substantial section of the population has its feet rooted in the camp of the Prime Minister Narendra Modi and his toxic political tradition (Hindutva), while a very large section – scattered around the country – has had its spirits lifted by the tenacity of the Indian farmers and agricultural workers.

In the summer of 2020, Modi's government pushed through three bills in the parliament that would effectively uberize the peasantry. This came after decades of cuts in subsidies and price supports to the farmers, which resulted – directly – in the deaths by suicide of 400,000 farmers, a fourth of them since Modi became prime minister in 2014. The farmers rightly saw Modi's three laws as an existential threat and so, on 26 November 2020, decided to be part of a general strike of 250 million workers and then stay in encampments around Delhi on an indefinite protest. This protest lasted through police repression, government hostility and attacks, and harsh weather (700 people died in the protest camps). On 19 November 2021, a week before the first anniversary of the protest, Modi surrendered and promised to withdraw the laws.

It is impossible to convey, in preçis, what this victory means. In his seven years in office, Modi has only backed down once before, and even then, to the farmers who fought off amendments to the Land Acquisition Act of 2013. Otherwise, Modi has been stubborn, unflinching even in the face of terrible violence in his name against Muslims (not only when he was chief minister of Gujarat in 2002, but also not far from his house during the Delhi pogrom of 2020).

There are immense problems before India. Even Modi's relatively pliant Niti Aayog (Policy Commission) concedes that about a quarter of India lives below the poverty line (around 350 million people). While China abolished absolute poverty in 2021, 75 million Indians slipped into poverty so that the estimated total now is at 134 million (an undercount); India's poor account for 30% of the world's poor. Poverty and hunger are at the heart of India's million crises and million mutinies. But these are not being addressed by the Modi government.

The victory of the farmers and the agricultural workers is a win not only for Indian democracy but for peasants around the world.

During the past five decades, peasants have experienced a combination of impoverishment, dispossession, and demoralisation on a global level. Two processes have accelerated their crisis: first, a trade and development model pushed by the advanced capitalist states through the International Monetary Fund (IMF), the World Bank, and the World Trade Organization (WTO); second, the climate catastrophe. The IMF's Structural Adjustment Programme and the WTO's liberalized trade regime have eroded price supports and food subsidies in the Global South and have prevented governments from intervening to assist farmers and to build robust national food markets (countries of the Global North, meanwhile, have continued to subsidize farming and dump their cheapened food in the markets of the Global South). This policy structure – alongside devastating climate events – has been fatal for agriculturalists in the Global South.

During the credit crisis of 2007-08, the World Bank intervened to promote the entry of the private sector (largely big agriculture) into the 'value chains' from farms to stores. 'The private sector drives the organization of value chains that bring the market to smallholders and commercial farms', wrote the World Bank in a key report from 2008. In June of that year, the UN Food and Agriculture Organization's High-Level Conference on World Food Security opened the door for the World Bank to shape agricultural policy to benefit big agriculture. The next year, the World Bank's World Development Report argued for integrating agriculture in the 'poor countries with world markets', which meant delivering the peasants into an uberized relationship with big agriculture (interestingly, the World Bank's own International Agricultural Assessment of Agricultural Knowledge, Science, and Technology disagreed in 2008, arguing that industrial agriculture degraded nature and impoverished peasants).

In September 2021, the UN held a Food Systems Summit in New York, which was designed not by farmers' unions but by the World Economic Forum (WEF), a private body that represents big business rather than the big hearts of the agriculturalists. Acknowledging the crisis imposed by capitalism, the WEF now says that it has learned from civil action and would like to promote 'stakeholder capitalism'. This new kind of capitalism, which looks like the old capitalism, is about promoting corporations as 'trustees of society'; it entrusts corporations with our well-being rather than the workers who produce the value in our society.

The farmers' revolt in India fought against Modi's three laws. But it continues to struggle against the transfer of policy making from democratic, multilateral, and national projects to corporations in the name of 'public-private partnerships' and 'trustees of society'. The repeal of Modi's laws is one victory. It has lifted the confidence of the people. But there are other battles ahead.

DOCUMENTING THE STRUGGLE

The farmers' revolt did not come out of nowhere. It was built by the farmers themselves, aware fully of the existential threat to their lives and livelihood because of the liberalization of agriculture and the commodification of agrarian society. They relied upon their own networks, links of community that became political in the heat of the policy changes coming from New Delhi. This radicalization was guided by the people's organizations – including the All-India Kisan Sabha (AIKS) and the All-India Agricultural Workers Union (AIAWU) – who provided their full strength into this difficult but important fight to defend the farmers and agricultural workers. The year-long revolt began during a peasant-worker general strike, which indicates the close links between the industrial trade union movement, the union movement of precarious care workers, and the formations of the peasantry.

Ashok Dhawale, the president of the AIKS, has been part of this struggle from the very first, before the 2015 struggle over the Land Acquisition Act, deep in the fight of the farmers of Maharashtra, and then in the historical year-long struggle against the attempt to uberize farm work across India. As the current wave of struggles grew, a range of farmer and agricultural worker organizations formed the Samyukta Kisan Morcha (United Farmers' Front – SKM), in which Comrade Dhawale emerged as a leader. He has not only helped shape the struggle, but he has – throughout the struggle – documented it, both its advances and its limitations. This book is the culmination of his documentation. It derives its analysis from Comrade Dhawale's proximity to this struggle, his key role as leader of honesty and humanity.

In November 2021, after Modi promised to repeal the three laws, I interviewed Comrade Dhawale. Farmers know what they want, he told me, and they have said so clearly: price supports, loan waivers, withdrawal of electricity price hikes, repeal of the labour codes, subsidized costs of fuel, and so on. These issues, Comrade Dhawale said, 'are at the root of the agrarian crisis and massive peasant indebtedness. They lead to farmer deaths by suicide and to distress sales of farmlands'. 'If farmers are to grow our food and people are to eat, then the demands of the farmers must be met', Comrade Dhawale told me. This is not just a cry for Indian farmers. The farmers in India remain in a struggle for farmers and people everywhere.

When Farmers Stood Up

1. Bliss Was it in That Dawn to be Alive

Bliss was it in that dawn to be alive,
But to be young was very heaven!

These were the ecstatic lines of the great British poet William Wordsworth, written to hail the beginning of the French Revolution. The very same emotions were stirred in my heart, and the hearts of countless others, by the magnificent and historic farmers' struggle, which made its indelible mark on our country and the world for over a year.

It was bliss indeed to be alive, to be a small part of this gigantic struggle, which had no equal since Indian Independence. Many of us were not so young, but the sheer tenacity and grit of the farmers that we saw indeed made us feel much younger, and hence in Wordsworth's heaven!

Along with innumerable others, it was my great good fortune to be a part of the collective leadership of the Samyukta Kisan Morcha (SKM) and of one of its major constituent organizations, the All India Kisan Sabha (AIKS), which together led this magnificent farmers' struggle for over a year. None of us had ever seen and experienced anything like it.

The unprecedented farmers' struggle that began at the borders of India's capital, Delhi, on 26 November 2020 and which won a famous victory over the reactionary forces of corporate communalism a full one year and fifteen days later on 11 December 2021, has been by far the largest, the longest, and the most powerful nationwide farmers' struggle in the history of India, and also in the world, with the exception of the momentous Chinese Revolution, which had to base itself on the peasantry. It succeeded in getting the three anti-farmer, anti-people, and pro-corporate – the three black Farm Laws – repealed. This struggle had several distinctive features.

NINE DISTINCTIVE FEATURES OF THE STRUGGLE

First, it was led by over 500 farmers' organizations, who had united under the platform of the SKM. This kind of broad issue-based unity among farmers' organizations was unprecedented in the history of India. Large sections of the peasantry came together across the nation and particularly at the Delhi borders – from agricultural workers to poor peasants to middle peasants and even some sections of rich peasants.

Second, it was fully supported by the Joint Platform of Central Trade Unions (CTUs) in the true spirit of worker-peasant unity. In fact, the struggle itself began as a joint struggle, with the *Chalo Delhi* call by farmers, and an All India Working Class Strike on the same day – 26 November 2020. Lakhs of peasants and workers from all over the country came out on the streets in solidarity with the farmers' struggle at the Delhi borders over the last year.

Third, it combated tremendous repression from the BJP-RSS-led central and state governments in the form of teargas shells, water cannons, dug up highways, massive barricades, lathi charges, wanton arrests, false police cases, and even farmers being mowed down by cars of a BJP Union Minister! But this struggle overcame it all. Over 715 farmers were martyred in the course of this battle in the last year. They included women and men, young and old.

Fourth, it faced constant defamation from the BJP-RSS combine and was ridiculously accused of being instigated by Khalistanis and Naxalites and Maoists, and even by Pakistan and China! As expected, sections of the corporate-owned 'Godi' media blurted out all these charges ad nauseam in typical Goebbelsian fashion, covering themselves with lasting shame. But the farmers' struggle consistently fought against all this defamation and valiantly stood its ground.

Fifth, it combated the worst health disaster to strike India and the world in recent times, the deadly Covid pandemic. The government suppressed the earlier big mass struggle against the

CAA-NRC-NPR in 2019-20 under the excuse of the pandemic. The farmers' struggle began in the pandemic and continued valiantly even through the disastrous second wave from April to June 2021. The government deliberately pushed through the Farm Laws during the Covid pandemic, thinking that no resistance would be possible. Farmers blew that illusion to smithereens.

Sixth, despite lakhs of farmers laying siege to Delhi for 380 days and nights, the struggle was entirely peaceful and democratic. It indeed adhered to Mahatma Gandhi's celebrated maxim: 'Truth and Non-Violence are as old as the hills'. It also victoriously combated the criminal conspiracy of violence unleashed by the BJP-RSS central government, its police and its agent provocateurs on 26 January 2021, Republic Day, at the time of the massive tractor rallies.

Seventh, it was entirely secular. The farmers' struggle over India cut across religion, caste, region, and language. It included men and women, and young and old. The contribution of women and youth in this movement was truly remarkable. The SKM began Mission Uttar Pradesh with a 10 lakh-strong rally at Muzaffarnagar, which had been the scene of terrible communal violence engineered by the BJP-RSS eight years ago. This secular and inclusive nature of class unity made it impossible for the government to suppress it.

Eighth, the political defeat of the BJP in the state assembly elections in Kerala, Tamil Nadu, and West Bengal; in the local body elections in Punjab and Uttar Pradesh; and in the parliamentary and assembly by-elections in Himachal Pradesh, Haryana, and Rajasthan, threw the BJP-RSS regime on the defensive in the run-up to the state assembly elections in Punjab, Uttar Pradesh and Uttarakhand. It was this fear that made it repeal the hated Farm Laws.

Ninth, and most importantly, this struggle directly identified and attacked the corrupt nexus of corporate communalism between the BJP-RSS-led central government and the Indian and foreign corporate lobby, symbolized by the Ambanis and Adanis.

The Modi regime also brought in these Farm Laws at the behest of US imperialism and the World Trade Organization (WTO). Through its three major demands, this massive class struggle of the peasantry, in fact, squarely attacked the neoliberal policies and imperialist dictates themselves.

WHY WERE THE FARM LAWS OPPOSED?

The farmers' struggle had three cardinal demands. First, the repeal of the three anti-farmer, anti-people, and pro-corporate Farm Laws. Second, the demand for a central law to ensure Minimum Support Price (MSP) and procurement at one-and-a-half times the comprehensive cost of production – a seminal recommendation of the National Commission on Farmers, headed by Dr M.S. Swaminathan. Third, the withdrawal of the Electricity Amendment Bill, which sought to privatize electricity and massively increase power tariffs across the board.

The first demand was the repeal of the three Farm Laws that were first promulgated as ordinances in June 2020, and were then rammed through Parliament in September 2020 after trampling on all democratic norms. No reference to a select committee was allowed. No amendments were allowed. No voting was allowed. Some Members of Parliament who resisted the passage of these Farm Laws were suspended. No Kisan organization worth its name had demanded any of these laws, and no Kisan organization was ever consulted. Although agriculture is a state subject under the Constitution, no state government was ever consulted either. As such, the Farm Laws were clearly unconstitutional.

The first Farm Act aimed to dismantle the Agricultural Produce Market Committees (APMCs) and hand over the entire trade in agricultural produce to domestic and foreign corporates. This would have destroyed farmers and agriculture, and would also have compromised the food security of the country. The Bihar state government under chief minister Nitish Kumar dismantled

APMCs in 2006. As a result, farmers in Bihar are getting around Rs 800 to Rs 1000 less per quintal of paddy than the MSP, which is now Rs 1940. This Act eventually aimed to do away with MSP and government procurement of food grains. The entire public distribution system (PDS) would have been dismantled with this. It would have hit 81 crores of both urban and rural poor, who avail the relatively cheap food grains from the PDS.

The second Farm Act aimed to encourage and promote contract farming across the country. As the previous experience of contract farming in India and the world shows, this would only help the powerful corporate companies to loot the farmers. In a travesty of justice, there was no provision for farmers for approaching courts in case of any dispute. There was also a real danger of the corporates swallowing up the land of the farmers in distress. The genuine alternative to corporate farming is co-operative farming, which the government is unwilling to consider.

The third Farm Act was a disastrous amendment to the Essential Commodities Act (ECA). The ECA had initially been adopted in 1955 to ensure the delivery of certain commodities or products, the supply of which, if obstructed through hoarding or black marketing, would affect the everyday life of the people. The central government now removed all restrictions on stocks of the six most essential items, viz. rice, wheat, pulses, cooking oil, onions, and potatoes. This would give the corporates and big traders a free hand to hoard and black market these essential items and hike their prices manifold. This would also endanger food security. In the Global Hunger Index figures declared recently, India already ranked 101 among 116 countries. This would aggravate even further.

ALL THREE PRODUCTIVE CLASSES ATTACKED

If we see the neoliberal direction of the Modi government's policies from the Shanta Kumar Committee recommendations of 2015 onwards, it will be apparent that these three Farm Laws were essentially meant to gradually dismantle the MSP regime, government procurement, storage of food grains in FCI godowns, and thus the entire PDS itself.

Eventually, this trajectory would also attack and seek to usurp the land of the peasantry in distress. An attempt was already made towards this end by the Modi regime through the Land Acquisition Amendment Ordinance of 2015. But that was defeated. However, many BJP state governments forced the same amendments through their state assemblies.

The BJP regime sought to hand over the entire agricultural sector to the domestic and foreign corporate lobby to increase its super-profits and its wealth. Within a fortnight of the enactment of the Farm Laws, 29 labour laws – that had been won by the working class after decades of bitter struggles – were annulled in Parliament and were replaced by four anti-worker Labour Codes. The employment lifeline of agricultural workers – the Mahatma Gandhi National Rural Employment Guarantee Act (MGNREGA) – was starved of funds.

The same classes that produce the wealth of the country through their labour – the workers, the peasants, and the agricultural workers – are thus being viciously attacked. This is the real meaning of corporate communalism, whose main symbols today are Narendra Modi, Amit Shah, Mukesh Ambani, and Gautam Adani. And this is the impending disaster against which the farmers' struggle waged an uncompromising battle for eighteen months – from June 2020, when the Farm Laws were first brought in as Ordinances, to December 2021, when the three Farm Laws were repealed.

In 1991, the Congress central government began the neoliberal policies in our country. They were then taken forward by all subsequent central governments and have been speeded up exponentially by the current Modi-led BJP-RSS regime. As a result, the agrarian crisis has reached alarming proportions in the last three decades of neoliberal policies.

As per the National Crime Records Bureau (NCRB) figures, over four lakh farmers have died by suicide due to indebtedness in the last 25 years, from 1995 to 2020. Of these, over one lakh farmers have been forced to commit suicide in the last eight years of the BJP regime alone. Lakhs of children of poor Adivasi, Dalit, and backward families die every year due to starvation. These are the two main symptoms of the agrarian crisis, which is aggravating year after year.

WHY ARE MSP AND PROCUREMENT SO CRUCIAL?

The second key demand of the farmers' struggle was for a law to guarantee MSP and procurement of all agricultural produce at one-and-a-half times the comprehensive cost of production (C2+50%), as recommended by the National Commission on Farmers, headed by the renowned agricultural scientist Dr M.S. Swaminathan. It was one of the promises in the BJP's election manifesto of 2014, repeated by Narendra Modi in his 400-odd speeches throughout the country as part of that election campaign.

But the very next year, in February 2015, the Modi government submitted an affidavit to the Supreme Court of India (SC), which said that it could not fulfil this promise because that would 'distort the market'. The Modi regime is now telling a white lie when it claims that it has already implemented MSP at this rate. It has applied the formula A2+FL, which is much lower than C2+50% and has thus tried to deceive farmers.

Moreover, in most parts of our country, the MSP declared by the central government for 23 different Kharif and Rabi season crops has no meaning, simply because there is no government procurement in most of the states. Hence traders routinely buy agricultural produce from farmers at much lower rates than the MSP. Even in Punjab, Haryana, and Western Uttar Pradesh, government procurement is restricted mainly to only paddy and wheat. Hence, the demand for a legal MSP guarantee is crucial for farmers.

The demand for a legal MSP guarantee assumes importance for the following major reasons:

First, successive central governments implementing neoliberal policies have increased the cost of production in agriculture manifold over the last three decades. One by slashing subsidies on agricultural inputs like fertilizers. Two, encouraging rapacious corporates to manufacture seeds, fertilizers, and insecticides – thus vastly increasing their price. Three, by massively increasing the price of diesel, petrol, power and irrigation. The cost of production in agriculture has indeed sky-rocketed.

Second, the price that the farmer gets for his crop has never increased in the same proportion. There are numerous instances where the price that the farmer gets is not even enough to cover the cost of production. Herein lies one of the primary roots of the agrarian crisis today – the massive peasant indebtedness leading to farmers dying by suicide on the one hand – and the distress sales of farmland on the other. The other basic root is the failure of successive central governments to carry out radical land reforms and distribute 'Land to the Tiller' and to the landless. This was one of the fundamental slogans of our freedom struggle. In the neoliberal era, this slogan has been replaced in practice with 'Land to the Corporates'.

Third, this is aggravated by natural calamities like severe droughts, floods, hailstorms, and unseasonal rains, with no proper crop insurance cover. These growing natural calamities have been directly related to global warming and climate change in recent years. Prime Minister Fasal Bima Yojana (PMFBY) has proved to be a farce – enriching corporate insurance companies – at the expense of the farmers and the central and state governments – all of whom shell out big premiums. Corporate insurance companies, while swallowing the premiums, refuse to compensate farmers for crop losses due to natural calamities, under one pretext or the other.

Fourth, as part of the neoliberal trajectory, the bank credit policy has been changed, and agriculture is no longer on the priority lending list like it was before. With vast amounts of even agricultural credit being channelized to corporate agri-businesses, there is a severe credit crunch in the farm sector, especially for small and middle farmers. This results in farmers being thrown to rapacious private money lenders, who charge interest rates between 24 and 60 per cent per annum. There is no chance that farmers can ever repay such exorbitant sums.

Fifth, the agricultural import-export policies adopted under WTO dictates and the various Free Trade Agreements (FTAs) have also hit farmers very hard. To give just one glaring example, the Modi government has slashed import duty on wheat to zero per cent. This had never been done before. It is a bonanza for the foreign corporates in the wheat trade. It recently reduced import duty on cotton. Similarly, FTAs have severely hit cash crops in Kerala and elsewhere, and the dairy sector all over the country.

It is for all these reasons, that the farmers' struggle has demanded a law to guarantee MSP and procurement at one-and-a-half times the comprehensive cost of production.

Another crucial demand of the peasant movement, in view of the alarming peasant deaths by suicide due to indebtedness, has been a complete loan waiver to the peasantry by the central government. Nationwide partial loan waivers to farmers had been implemented twice before by central governments. The first was in 1990 by the National Front government led by V.P. Singh. The second was in 2008 by the UPA-1 government led by Manmohan Singh.

But the BJP-RSS government led by Narendra Modi has dismissed the demand for loan waiver by farmers out of hand – despite having promised that, too, in the 2014 elections. However, the same regime has no hesitation in writing off bank loans to the tune of Rs 10.72 lakh crore to a handful of its favourite crony corporates over the last seven years. This is in addition to the astronomical tax concessions this government gives every year to the corporate lobby.

The third demand of this struggle was the withdrawal of the Electricity Amendment Bill 2020, which shamelessly promotes further privatization of power and aims to end cross-subsidy. This will lead to a massive hike in power bills not only for irrigation pumps of farmers, but also for domestic use in both rural and urban areas. It will hit all the working people.

TRUE SIGNIFICANCE OF THE FARMERS' STRUGGLE

Today the entire country is being put up for sale through the government's anti-national policy of reckless privatization of the public sector, and the National Monetization Pipeline. The nakedly pro-corporate policies of the Modi-led BJP-RSS government are aimed at selling off the entire country under cover of the hypocritical slogan of '*atmanirbharata*' (self-reliance).

There is no area of the public sector that the Modi regime has not put up for privatization and sale to Indian and foreign corporates in the last eight years of its rule – be it railways, airlines, airports, ports, mines, steel, coal, oil, telecom, banks, insurance, irrigation, power, education, health, and even defence. Now it is agriculture and land which is on its hit list. And this was bitterly opposed by the farmers' struggle.

The true significance of this farmers' struggle throughout the country was that it struck squarely at these disastrous and anti-national policies of the BJP-RSS regime, which has always acted as the most servile agent of the feudal, corporate and imperialist lobby, right from the days of our freedom struggle. The farmers' struggle struck a mighty blow for democracy and secularism. It was a patriotic struggle waged by millions of farmers not only for themselves – but also in defence of the people and the entire country.

2. THE GENESIS OF THE FARMERS' STRUGGLE

The farmers' struggle of 2020-21 did not suddenly emerge out of the blue. It was not a spontaneous struggle that cropped up out of nowhere. On the contrary, it was the culmination of several powerful nationwide and statewide peasant struggles that steadily intensified after 2014, when the Modi-led BJP-RSS regime came to power at the centre. These struggles realized that this BJP-RSS central government was the worst culprit in intensifying neoliberal policies in agriculture, thus attacking the peasantry. BJP-led state governments also followed suit.

The last eight years saw a constant strengthening of peasant resistance against the neoliberal assault on their livelihoods by the Modi government. As agrarian distress intensified due to these assaults, peasants and agricultural workers, along with the working class, strongly raised their voices against it. Let us look at the major agrarian protests in the years after 2014.

STRUGGLE AGAINST LAND ACQUISITION AMENDMENT ORDINANCE – 2015

Till 2013, land acquisition was governed by the archaic and reactionary Land Acquisition Act enacted by the British colonial regime way back in 1894. It took a full 119 years after that – which was 66 years after independence – for the Right to Fair Compensation and Transparency in Land Acquisition, Rehabilitation and Resettlement Act, 2013 (briefly known as the LARR Act, 2013) to be enacted in Parliament under the UPA-2 regime after fairly comprehensive consultation. Although some problems remained, the 2013 Act was a substantial advance over the 1894 Act.

But as soon as the Modi government came to power, on 31 December 2014, it brought in a thoroughly reactionary Ordinance to amend the LARR Act of 2013. The thrust of this Ordinance was clearly pro-corporate and anti-farmer, making it much easier for the corporates and their governments to acquire land from farmers. It clearly was a Land Grab Ordinance.

A nationwide peasant struggle began in February 2015 against this reactionary Ordinance. It was led by the Bhumi Adhikar Andolan (BAA), a joint platform in which the All India Kisan Sabha (AIKS) played a vital role along with the National Alliance of People's Movements (NAPM) and over 100 other peasant organizations. The Ordinance was publicly burnt in large actions in over 300 districts across the country. Two large peasant marches to Parliament were held under the BAA banner condemning the Ordinance, the first on 24 February 2015 and the second on 5 May 2015. The BAA organized a public hearing on the issue on 23 July 2015.

At that time, the BJP was in a minority in the Rajya Sabha, and Left Members of Parliament (MP) rallied the entire opposition to oppose this Ordinance. The Bihar state assembly elections were also around the corner. All this forced the Modi regime to withdraw the hated Ordinance on 31 August 2015 eventually. This was the first significant policy defeat of the new BJP-RSS government, and it was farmers who inflicted it. However, several BJP state governments later pushed Bills making amendments similar to this Ordinance through their state assemblies.

NATIONWIDE JATHAS AND PARLIAMENT MARCH – 2016

As the agrarian crisis started intensifying, in November 2016, the AIKS organized four impressive nationwide vehicle jathas throughout the country. The nationwide jathas travelled over 20,000 km through 18 states of the country. Hundreds of public meetings were held in which a total of over one lakh peasants participated. They focused on the burning issues of peasant loan waiver, remunerative MSP, land rights, enhanced pensions, and

MGNREGA expansion. They culminated in a large AIKS rally before Parliament on 24 November 2016. The savage attack of demonetization took place when the jathas were on. Surmounting even that, tens of thousands of peasants from the country came to Delhi to make the rally a great success.

UNITED FARMERS' STRIKE FOR LOAN WAIVER IN MAHARASHTRA – 2017

On 1 June 2017, after considerable preparation, a novel united farmers' strike began in Maharashtra for loan waiver and remunerative prices. Farmers stopped getting their milk, vegetables, and fruits for sale in the cities in an unprecedented move. On 3 June, some of the leaders of the strike, while negotiating with the BJP chief minister Devendra Fadnavis, sold out. Without getting anything concrete in hand, they decided to withdraw the strike. At this point, AIKS state general secretary, Dr Ajit Nawale, who was part of the negotiations with the chief minister, walked out, announced the betrayal to the media, and declared the resolve of the farmers to continue the strike until a loan waiver was wrested.

The AIKS leadership mobilized other farmers' organizations to continue the strike, and this effort bore fruit. Dr Ajit Nawale was elected as the convenor of the coordination committee leading the strike. A massive Maharashtra Bandh to support the farmers' strike was held on 5 June. A convention was held at Nashik on 8 June. It called for a statewide Rail Roko agitation on 13 June. The momentum of the farmers' strike increased with every passing day.

On 11 June, under this pressure, the BJP state government was forced to bend. It called the coordination committee for talks. It initially agreed to a complete loan waiver to the peasantry. Later, it went back on its word and imposed several conditions. The chief minister declared a Rs 34,000 crore loan waiver package of Rs 1.5 lakh each to 89.87 lakh peasants out of 1.36 crore peasants in the state. However, due to the onerous conditions imposed, by

December 2019, the loan waiver had benefited 44.23 lakh farmers who got a loan waiver of Rs 19,843 crore. Although lakhs of peasants were left out, even this was a significant achievement.

The struggle for extending the loan waiver continued even later, and the Maha Vikas Aghadi (MVA) state government that came to power in November 2019 increased the loan waiver amount to Rs 2 lakh each and expanded the ambit of the scheme. Till December 2021, 31.71 lakh farmers received the additional benefit of loan waiver amounting to Rs 20,243 crore.

Thus, in the five years from 2017 to 2021, farmers in Maharashtra succeeded in wresting a total loan waiver of more than Rs 40,000 crore through their struggle.

STRUGGLE FOR LOAN WAIVER AND PENSION HIKE IN RAJASTHAN – 2017

Rajasthan had seen vast struggles of the peasantry led by the AIKS even before 2014. The most impressive was the eight-day long victorious statewide *mahapadav* (mega sit-in) in Jaipur on the electricity issue in 2005. In 2017, the AIKS began a statewide struggle on an 11-point demand charter which included loan waiver, cancellation of toll tax on highways, increase in pensions, and other issues. After a series of local struggles, a ten-day *mahapadav* of thousands of peasants was held at the grain market in Sikar from 1 to 10 September 2017. When the BJP state government refused to relent – a state-wide, three-day road blockade was held from 11-13 September. Peasant women took part in the struggle in a big way, and it was led by AIKS leaders Amra Ram, Chhagan Lal Choudhary, Pema Ram, Sanjay Madhav, and many others.

Under the pressure of this struggle, the BJP state government led by Vasundhara Raje Scindia was forced to relent and invite the AIKS for talks. In a written agreement, the government waived farmers' loans up to Rs 50,000 each, cancelled the toll tax on state highways, agreed to give pensions to farmers above 60 years of age, and scholarship dues to SC–ST students.

Another struggle had to be launched in February 2018 since the BJP government was dragging its feet on implementing the agreement. The AIKS gave a call for a statewide protest march to Jaipur on 22 February 2018. To pre-empt this, the government began large scale arrests of farmer leaders from 20 February. Thousands of peasants hit back by blocking the Sikar-Jaipur highway for three days. As a result, the government was forced to release all the arrested leaders and declare that the 2017 agreement would be implemented.

KISAN MUKTI SANSAD FOR LOAN WAIVER AND MSP – 2017

When the above mentioned Maharashtra farmers' strike was in progress, farmers from Mandsaur in Madhya Pradesh began their own struggle for loan waiver and remunerative prices. On 6 June 2017, the BJP state government of Madhya Pradesh resorted to brutal police firing, killing six farmers. Farmers across the country widely condemned this in demonstrations on 16 June.

Soon after this firing, several farmers' organizations came together to form the All India Kisan Sangharsh Coordination Committee (AIKSCC), with the AIKS and other organizations being its major constituents. After a countrywide Kisan Mukti Yatra traversed several states, the AIKSCC held an impressive Kisan Mukti Sansad and Mahila Kisan Sansad in Delhi on 20-21 November 2017. Thousands of farmers participated in it from across the country.

The 'Farmers' Freedom from Indebtedness Bill' was presented before the Kisan Mukti Sansad by AIKS general secretary Hannan Mollah, former MP. And the 'Farmers' Right to Guaranteed Remunerative Minimum Support Prices for Agricultural Commodities Bill' was presented by Raju Shetti, MP. These two seminal AIKSCC Bills were then finalized after extensive countrywide consultations. They were then placed before Parliament as private members' bills in August 2018 by AIKS joint secretary K.K. Ragesh in the Rajya Sabha and Raju Shetti in the Lok Sabha. Both these bills were supported by leaders of 21 opposition parties in a convention in New Delhi.

KISAN LONG MARCH IN MAHARASHTRA – 2018

The AIKS-led iconic Kisan Long March on foot in Maharashtra from Nashik to Mumbai from 6-12 March 2018 electrified the country. It was an amazing struggle. It caught the imagination of the peasantry and the people, receiving unstinted support all over the country. It received the backing of parties and organizations all across the political spectrum. For the week that the Kisan Long March of nearly 200 km lasted, it became the centre of attraction for the entire national and state media, both print and electronic, and also social media. #KisanLongMarch was the number one trending All-India hashtag the whole day on 12 March.

Beginning at Nashik with over 25,000 farmers marching in unison, including thousands of peasant women, it concluded in Mumbai with over 50,000 farmers. Red flags of the Kisan Sabha, red banners, red caps, and red placards highlighting the main demands of this Long March made it a colossal ocean of red. The magnificent humanitarian decision of the AIKS of walking day and night on the last day, from 11 am on 11 March to 6 am on 12 March, from Thane city to Azad Maidan in the heart of Mumbai city, to avoid disrupting the final board examinations of tens of thousands of SSC students in Mumbai, drew the unstinted admiration of people across the country. Several prominent celebrities also expressed their appreciation.

By far, the largest mobilization in this march was that of thousands of Adivasi peasants from Nashik district. The next was from Thane-Palghar district, followed by Ahmednagar district. There was representation from several other districts in the state too, which rose markedly in the last three days of the Long March. This March was the culmination of three years of constant struggles led by the AIKS in Maharashtra. AIKS leaders J.P. Gavit (MLA), Kisan Gujar, Dr Ajit Nawale, myself, and others led the Kisan Long March.

The BJP state government was forced to bend before this decisive mass struggle. Concrete time-bound written assurances were given by the government on AIKS demands. These demands were: the implementation of the Forest Rights Act (FRA); the river linking proposal adversely affecting tribals in Nashik, Palghar and Thane districts; increase of loan waiver to farmers; a mechanism for remunerative prices; vesting of temple lands; regularizing houses on pasture lands; no land acquisition without consent; increase in old-age pensions; improving the public distribution system; and compensation to lakhs of farmers in the Vidarbha and Marathwada regions who had suffered huge losses of the cotton crop due to pink bollworm pest attacks, hailstorms, and so on. The agreement was reached on 12 March between the Government of Maharashtra and the AIKS. The next day, it was tabled in both houses of the Maharashtra legislature.

CITU-AIKS-AIAWU JAIL BHARO AND MARCH TO PARLIAMENT – 2018

The unprecedented success of the 9 August 2018 nationwide Jail Bharo struggle, which mobilized over five and a half lakh people, and the 5 September 2018 Mazdoor Kisan Sangharsh Rally in Delhi, which mobilized over two lakh people, were two striking examples of the rising wave of united worker-peasant struggles over the last few years. Both these struggles were led under the Red Flag jointly by three class organizations – All India Kisan Sabha (AIKS), Centre of Indian Trade Unions (CITU), and All India Agricultural Workers Union (AIAWU).

The 9 August Jail Bharo struggle mobilized 5.5 lakh peasants and workers, at over 610 centres in 407 districts in 23 states. The peasants led by AIKS were around 3 lakh, the workers led by CITU were about 2 lakh, and agricultural workers led by AIAWU were around 50 thousand. The largest participation in the 5 September Delhi Rally to Parliament was of the CITU and industrial federations, followed by the AIKS and AIAWU. The national capital Delhi had turned red. On the previous day, 4 September, over 10,000 women led by the All India Democratic Women's Association (AIDWA) held a similar nationwide march to Parliament, braving drenching rain.

The two significant struggles of 9 August and 5 September illustrated worker-peasant unity in action at the national level. They represented the unity of the three basic classes and the toiling people who actually produce the wealth of our country through their labour. Both these struggles created tremendous enthusiasm at all levels throughout the country. This was reflected in the participation of several lakhs that they achieved. One important characteristic of both these actions was the massive participation of women and youth.

Both these actions were directed against the anti-people, pro-corporate, neoliberal policies of the BJP-RSS central government led by Prime Minister Narendra Modi. They also castigated the communal, casteist, corrupt, and authoritarian trends of the Modi regime. They channelized the rapidly growing discontent and anger of the people against the rulers and also, to an extent, put forth alternative policies based on a 15-point charter of demands of all three basic classes. These struggles had a significant political impact at both the national and the state levels.

The 5 September rally gave two major action calls for the future. One was to participate in full-strength in the AIKSCC-organized united Kisan Mukti March to Delhi on 29-30 November 2018. The second was to participate in strength in the two-day All India general strike of the working class on 8-9 January 2019, as per the call of the joint trade union convention held in Delhi.

AIKSCC KISAN MUKTI MARCH TO PARLIAMENT – 2018

Another major initiative was the AIKSCC-led countrywide Kisan Mukti March to Parliament on 29-30 November 2018. It began from five points near Delhi on 29 November 2018. Thousands of farmers walked a distance of 15-20 km to the Ramlila Maidan from these points. They enjoyed an impressive cultural night in the evening – *Ek Sham Kisano Ke Naam*.

On 30 November, around one lakh farmers began a massive march from Ramlila Maidan. It reached Parliament at noon. It was a microcosm of rural India. Poor and middle farmers, tenant farmers, agricultural workers, fisherfolk, and even some wealthy farmers were part of this rally. Women farmers, Adivasi farmers, Dalit farmers, farmers from minority communities were also present in large numbers. Every participant had a story of hardship – and resistance – to share. Many sections of the media captured these anecdotes.

It was a heart-rending sight to see wives and daughters of farmers from Telangana walking in the rally with framed photographs of their husbands and fathers who had died by suicide due to indebtedness. Farmers from Tamil Nadu had come with the skulls and bones of their farmer brethren, who had died by suicide.

The Kisan Mukti March castigated the BJP-RSS central government for its anti-farmer policies, and demanded that the two private members' bills for loan waiver and remunerative MSP placed in Parliament on behalf of the AIKSCC in August 2018 be discussed and adopted. It demanded a special session of Parliament to discuss the agrarian crisis and related issues. It also adopted a 19-point Manifesto of Indian Farmers which included the demands of all agrarian sections, including agricultural workers, fisherfolk, and so on. (See Appendix 2.)

The nationwide farmers' struggle of 2020-21 was the climax of all these earlier massive peasant struggles and campaigns. Many other state-level peasant struggles also took place during this period around various issues. But space does not permit a recounting of all of them.

Over the years, the implementation of the Swaminathan Commission's recommendation of remunerative MSP at one-and-a-half times the comprehensive cost of production (C2+50%), and freedom from debt became the two main demands of the peasantry. The demand to increase the guaranteed days of work under MGNREGA to 200, wages to Rs 600, and a similar Urban Employment Guarantee Scheme, also became an important demand.

It was in this background that the introduction of the three black Farm Laws became the proverbial last straw. After the Modi government promulgated the three Farm Laws first as ordinances on 5 June 2020, the AIKSCC gave a countrywide call for mass protests. Several other Kisan organizations in Punjab also began a struggle, and they later formed a joint front of 32 farmers' organizations, including the AIKS. The BKU (Ekta Ugrahan), perhaps the largest farmers' organization in Punjab, chose not to be a part of these 32 organizations but began its independent struggle on the same issues. But it later joined the SKM.

When the Modi regime rammed through the three Farm Laws in Parliament in September 2020 by murdering parliamentary democracy and attacking the federal principle, the AIKSCC gave a clarion call for countrywide actions on 25 September 2020. This mobilized lakhs of farmers all over the country, and it turned into a Bandh in Punjab, Haryana and some other states. The AIKSCC also gave a call for a massive *Chalo Delhi* on 26 November 2020.

BIRTH OF THE SKM

On 26-27 October 2020, the AIKSCC invited other farmers' organizations from Punjab, Haryana and other states outside its fold to a joint meeting in Delhi. Many of these organizations go by the name of the Bharatiya Kisan Union (BKU), a farmers' organization that was originally formed many decades ago by Choudhary Charan Singh and later reconstituted by Mahendra Singh Tikait. They add the suffix of their leader or village in brackets. The Rashtriya Kisan Mahasangh (RKM) and its constituent organizations were invited a little later. Organizations like the BKU (Tikait) in Uttar Pradesh joined the struggle and the SKM soon after.

The grave danger that the three Farm Laws posed to the peasantry and the people was recognized by all. The need to forge a broad unity of all farmers' organizations against the BJP-RSS regime, its crony corporates and the World Trade Organization (WTO), all of whom had forced these Farm Laws, was also realized by all.

It was in these meetings in October 2020 that the SKM was born. It was an unprecedented development – 500 farmers' organizations coming together against a common enemy. The SKM unitedly led the year-long farmers' struggle from 26 November 2020 to 11 December 2021.

Ideologically, the organizations in the SKM belonged to the left, right, and centre. But it was indeed a welcome development that they all came together in an issue-based struggle. Herculean efforts by many went into building this unprecedented unity of farmers' organizations. But in the final analysis – this unity led to victory.

All the decisions in this year-long struggle were taken in SKM meetings that were held in the showroom of Kajaria Tiles at Singhu border. These meetings were regularly attended by over 200 leaders representing various organizations in the SKM. Towards the beginning of the struggle, after making various changes, a 9-member SKM coordination committee was formed. It made proposals to the wider SKM meeting, whose decisions were always final and binding.

This 9-member coordination committee of the SKM comprised the following: Balbir Singh Rajewal, Dr Darshan Pal, Gurnam Singh Charuni, Hannan Mollah, Jagjit Singh Dallewal, Joginder Singh Ugrahan, Shivkumar Sharma 'Kakaaji', Yudhvir Singh, and Yogendra Yadav.

Many of the SKM meetings were naturally stormy, given the wide ideological and organizational differences among SKM constituents. But it is a great tribute to their collective maturity that all decisions were arrived at not by voting but through consensus.

For over 12 months, tens of thousands of farmers laid siege to the national capital at its borders like – Singhu, Tikri, Ghazipur, Shahajahanpur, Palwal and Mewat. They braved the bitter cold, scorching heat, and torrential rains, apart from all the repression, the defamation, and the pandemic. The struggle spread to almost all states across the country, where thousands of farmers and workers came onto the roads several times during this one year.

It is this struggle that ended in a monumental victory with the repeal of the three hated Farm Laws.

3 BJP-RSS REGIME WAGES WAR AGAINST ITS OWN FARMERS

Nothing like this was ever seen since Independence. A government waging war against its own people. Its own farmers. The *annadatas* (food-providers) of our country.

But that is precisely what the BJP-RSS governments and their police – both at the Centre and in Haryana – did. They directed the force of water cannons on the farmers of Punjab and Haryana. They slapped a murder charge on a youth farmer who climbed up the tanker and switched off the water cannons. They attacked farmers with innumerable tear gas shells. They resorted to brutal lathi charges. They arrested hundreds of farmer activists. They put up huge barricades and barbed wire fencings. They even dug up wide and deep trenches on the national highways to stop the advance of the farmers to the national capital Delhi. The notorious BJP-RSS government of Uttar Pradesh also cracked down on the farmers coming to Delhi from there.

Ironically, all this happened on 26 November 2020. 26 November is celebrated as Constitution Day. On this day in 1949, the Constituent Assembly adopted the Constitution of our country, which characterized our nation as being a 'sovereign, socialist, secular democratic republic'. The basic democratic tenet of dissent was trampled upon with fascistic fervour.

The repression of the government was intense. The resistance of the peasantry was incredible.

INTENSE REPRESSION, INCREDIBLE RESISTANCE

Tens of thousands of valiant farmers literally broke through this seemingly impregnable wall of repression erected by the government at both the Punjab-Haryana and Haryana-Delhi borders. They comprised young and old, women and men, of all religions and castes, in massive numbers. Their numbers, and their determination, were their real strength. They came in thousands of tractors and trollies. And they came with provisions enough to last for months. The defining moment of this remarkable peasant struggle came when these farmers came forward to feed the same police personnel who had rained blows of repression on them.

Confronted with this remarkable resistance, the central government was forced to surrender. It announced that the farmers could finally enter Delhi. All its actions so far were meant to prevent just that. It designated a large ground in Burari where farmers could come and camp.

And then came the master stroke. Tens of thousands of farmers just refused to enter Delhi. They decided to remain on the two major national highways on the Haryana-Delhi border, at Singhu and Tikri. Several kilometres of the national highways at both points were occupied by farmers, their tractors and their trollies. Asked why they were doing this when the government had given them permission to come into Delhi, a young farmer unerringly replied, 'We will not go to the ground in Burari because once we go there, we'll just sit there for years and nothing will happen. Here, the border is locked, and it will make an impact'.

When I visited Singhu border and saw this spectacle, I was immediately reminded of our *mahapadav* struggle in Maharashtra six years ago. On 29-30 March 2016, over one lakh farmers under the AIKS banner gathered at the huge Golf Club Maidan in Nashik. After the massive public meeting, which was addressed by Sitaram Yechury, Hannan Mollah, and P. Sainath, among others, we led the huge mass out to the main square in Nashik and blocked it for two days and two nights. All top government and police authorities were persuading us to go back to the Golf Club Maidan and continue our agitation. We refused for the same reason that the young farmer from Punjab gave. The entire city of Nashik was locked. Within 12 hours, the then BJP chief minister was forced to invite the AIKS delegation for talks in Mumbai.

The central government had given 3 December as the date for talks, under the illusion that the struggle would fizzle out by then. When it became evident that no such thing would happen, Union Home Minister Amit Shah set the condition that the government would hold talks only if the agitating farmers went into the Burari ground. The farmers spurned his offer with the contempt that it deserved. Eventually, the government was forced to bend and hold the first round of talks on 1 December.

But Prime Minister Narendra Modi had already queered the pitch for the talks by his recent 'Mann ki Baat', where he vigorously defended the three Farm Laws and declared yet again that they were beneficial for farmers at the precise time when lakhs of farmers had laid siege to the nation's capital for the scrapping of these very laws. As expected, the talks were inconclusive. It was clear from the obdurate response of the rulers that the struggle would be a long haul.

MAGNIFICENT WORKING-CLASS STRIKE

The magnificent 26 November All India Strike led by the CTUs, which was responded to by millions of workers, both organized and unorganized, and by middle-class employees, was a tight slap in the face of the BJP-RSS regime. On top of that came this farmers' struggle on the borders of the nation's capital itself. The cardinal importance of this November struggle was that it was a manifestation of worker-peasant unity in action. Both the working class and the peasantry of India supported each other's demands against their common enemy, the BJP-RSS central government and its alliance with the corporate lobby. The November struggle of the working class and the peasantry also proved yet again that it is only a united class struggle that can effectively combat communal, casteist and divisive conspiracies.

4. MAGNIFICENT BHARAT BANDH

BACKS FARMERS' CAUSE

It was a Bharat Bandh, the like of which had not been seen for the last several years. The Bandh called on 8 December 2020 by the SKM to support the nationwide struggle of farmers for the repeal of the three hated Farm Laws received a magnificent and spontaneous response from the people all over the country.

SIGNIFICANCE OF THE BHARAT BANDH

The Bandh was announced on the evening of 4 December. Three days were enough to galvanize the entire country into action against the pro-corporate and anti-farmer BJP-RSS regime.

The upsurge of farmers from North India, combined with the unprecedented nationwide working-class strike and peasant road blockades on 26 November, the countrywide farmers' demonstrations on 3 December, the burning of effigies of Modi, Shah, Ambani and Adani in several parts of the country on 5 December, set the stage for the Bharat Bandh on 8 December.

The Bharat Bandh showed great anger amongst the people against the massive repression unleashed by the government against farmers from Punjab and Haryana. It manifested the country's support to its *annadatas* who were fighting against the injustice heaped on them by a government that was clearly acting at the behest of its super-rich corporate masters. It also illustrated the massive unity of the people, transcending the barriers of religion, caste and language.

WIDESPREAD SUPPORT

The five Left parties – CPI(M), CPI, CPI(ML-L), RSP, and FB

– were the first to issue a statement on 5 December supporting the Bharat Bandh. They were followed by 20 other national and regional opposition parties. Except for the Bharatiya Mazdoor Sangh (BMS), all the central trade unions supported the Bandh call. Several organizations of agricultural workers, women, youth, students, and others came out in support.

Lakhs of activists of over 500 Kisan organizations which had come together under the umbrella of the SKM, and also those of the above political parties and class and mass organizations, came out on the streets and organized massive road and rail blockades, and held huge demonstrations in thousands of places across the country on the Bandh day.

Numerous organizations of traders, shopkeepers, and transporters supported the Bandh by downing their shutters and closing their fleets of vehicles. Several lawyers associations and bar councils passed resolutions supporting the farmers' cause. There was a churning in large sections of the middle class as well, with thousands expressing their support. Mainstream media was forced to sit upright for once and take notice. Social media covered it widely and vibrantly.

For the first time in seven years, the farmers' upsurge squarely threw the Modi regime on the defensive.

HUMANITARIAN LANGAR CULTURE

One of the things that impressed me the most in this struggle was the langar culture of the Sikhs. The Gurudwaras played a key role in it. Free food was served to anyone who wanted it. There were scores of langars functioning at all the Delhi borders. It must be stressed that this was one of the key reasons why this magnificent struggle could last for over a year. I was reminded of our Kisan Long March, when people of all religions and castes in Mumbai rushed to give food, water, and even new chappals, to the peasant men and women who had marched so bravely for a week.

The langar culture was not limited to the Delhi borders of this struggle alone. When around a thousand peasants from Maharashtra came in a vehicle march from Nashik to Delhi during the first month of the struggle in December 2020, we were accommodated and served food in two Gurudwaras at Kota and Jaipur in Rajasthan. We held two massive statewide Kisan Mazdoor Mahapanchayats in Mumbai – the first on 25 January 2021 and the second on 28 November 2021. In these Mahapanchayats, food to tens of thousands of participants was served free by the Gurudwaras of Mumbai and New Mumbai. It was simply amazing.

GROWING RADICALIZATION

The Bharat Bandh day, 8 December, was the thirteenth day of the mahapadav of lakhs of farmers from Punjab and Haryana at the Singhu and Tikri borders of Delhi. These two national highways had been closed down from 27 November. After that, thousands of farmers from Uttar Pradesh, Uttarakhand, and Madhya Pradesh almost closed down two other national highways coming to Delhi as they camped at the Ghazipur and Palwal borders. Rajasthan was in the midst of local body elections till 8 December. Farmers from Rajasthan and Haryana blocked the fifth remaining national highway, coming to Delhi from Jaipur, from 13 December at Shahjahanpur.

The mood of the farmers at all the places where they had congregated on the borders of Delhi had to be seen to be believed. There was a carnival atmosphere. Flags and banners of all Kisan organizations – red, green, gold, yellow, blue, white – mingled in unprecedented unity and camaraderie. That was the most distinctive feature of this farmers' struggle. Tractors and trollies were parked for several kilometres along the highways.

Public meetings were held from 11 am to 3 pm at the Delhi border protest sites daily throughout the one year and fifteen days of this struggle. Thousands of farmers attended them every day.

They were addressed by hundreds of activists of all the farmers' organizations. There was tremendous anger against the BJP-RSS regime led by Modi and Shah and against their crony corporates like Ambani and Adani. This was evident in the speeches of leaders, the reactions of farmers, and also the imaginative posters and placards that were everywhere.

There were cartoons sharply ridiculing Modi, Shah, Yogi, Khattar, Tomar, and also Ambani and Adani. Some of the cartoons inevitably compared Modi to Hitler. There were many catchy slogans based on the farmers' struggle. One of the most telling was – 'No Farmers! No Food! No Future!'. Another one was – 'We are Farmers! Not Terrorists!'

The countrywide call of the SKM to boycott Ambani and Adani products and services struck a chord and was well responded to in Punjab, Haryana, and other states. Farmers and other sections of the people led large demonstrations outside Reliance and Adani outlets in many states. Social media channels were used in a big way to popularize this campaign.

Another characteristic was the growing radicalization of the farmers in struggle at all the Delhi borders. In several places, we saw photo posters of Bhagat Singh, Dr Babasaheb Ambedkar, Chandrashekhar Azad, Kartar Singh Sarabha, and in a few places, even Marx, Lenin, and Che!

5. THE SUPREME COURT AND THE FARM LAWS

The Supreme Court of India (SC), after hearing a clutch of petitions on the farmers' struggle but completely ignoring the ones that challenged the constitutionality of the three Farm Laws on the grounds of the federal principle, criticized the central government for its handling of the farmers' struggle on 11 January 2021 and suspended the implementation of the Farm Laws 'until further notice' on 12 January.

But this was nullified by its constitution of a four-member committee comprised of government yes-men, all of whom had publicly supported the Farm Laws and were clear votaries of neoliberal policies and the corporate invasion of Indian agriculture. The four names were Ashok Gulati, Anil Ghanwat, Bhupinder Singh Mann, and Pramod Joshi. Bhupinder Singh Mann himself opted out of the committee within a few days. What recommendations such a committee would make could easily be surmised even before it began its work.

This made it crystal clear on which side the SC really stood. This was hardly surprising, given its record over the last few years. Crucial cases challenging the constitutional validity of the CAA, the abolition of Article 370, the withdrawal of statehood to Jammu and Kashmir, the draconian provisions of the UAPA, the crony corporate issue of electoral bonds which vitiated the free and fair electoral process, were all kept on the back burner for years. Bail for the Bhima Koregaon detainees was denied, while Arnab Goswami got bail in double-quick time.

SKM REJECTS SC COMMITTEE EVEN BEFORE ITS FORMATION

The SKM declared in its press release on 11 January, even before the SC announced the names of the committee, that it was 'not willing to participate in any proceedings before a committee that may be appointed by the Hon'ble Supreme Court'. On 12 January, after the announcement of the committee, the SKM, while reiterating that it would not participate in any such committee process, said, 'One of our apprehensions about such a process got validated in the very constitution of the committee. It is clear that the Court is being misguided by various forces even in its constitution of a committee. These are people who are known for their support for the three Farm Acts and have actively advocated for the same. It is not out of place to remember that the farmer unions have rejected a committee proposal from the government too. Our dialogue is basically with an elected government about its policy directions and concomitant laws'.

The SKM, in its statement, hit out hard against the Government of India (GOI) and its three Farm Acts, 'Farmers have explained in detail to GOI that the three Farm Laws will lead to corporate control over agricultural production, processing and markets. It will lead to high cost of inputs, higher debts on peasants, lower crop prices, increased farmer losses, decrease in government procurement, an end of the PDS, raised food costs, increased farmer and agricultural worker deaths by suicide, hunger deaths, and eviction from land due to debts. The Government has hidden these hard facts from the people and the courts'. It then reiterated its future programme of struggle.

SC COMMITTEE DOES WHAT WAS EXPECTED

The SC-appointed committee submitted its report in due course, but it was made public only in March 2022 – after the Uttar Pradesh, Punjab, Uttarakhand, and other assembly election results. Its recommendations were exactly what the SKM had expected.

After falsely asserting that 86 per cent of the farmers of India supported the three Farm Laws, a mention of some of the key recommendations of the committee will further expose its bias:

'A repeal or a long suspension of these Farm Laws would be

unfair to the 'silent' majority who support the Farm Laws.

'States may be allowed some flexibility in implementation and design of the Laws, with the prior approval of the Centre, so that the basic spirit of these Laws for promoting effective competition in agricultural markets and creation of 'one nation, one market' is not violated.

'The Government should consider in favour of completely abolishing the Essential Commodities Act, 1955, or take steps to substantially liberalize its provisions.

'The MSP and procurement support policy, as was designed for cereals during the Green Revolution time, needs to be revisited.

'For wheat and rice, there has to be a cap on procurement which is commensurate to the needs of the Public Distribution System (PDS).

'The procurement of crops at a declared MSP can be the prerogative of the States as per their specific agricultural policy priorities.'

The AIKS, in its statement released on 22 March 2022, denounced all these recommendations.

ARMY VETERANS RETURN GALLANTRY MEDALS

In a very significant move, as reported by *The Hindu* on 13 December, Army veterans from Punjab and Haryana who were camping at Singhu border collected over 5,000 gallantry medals since 26 November to return to the central government. Some extracts from this report were eye-openers.

80 year-old retired Havaldar Balwant Singh from Jhajjar in Haryana said, 'I come from a family of jawans and kisans, which have eight martyrs, either in war or at the border. I was proud of that fact, but because of what the government is doing now, it has begun feeling like this country is no longer worth living in, leave alone to die for. We have been here since 26 November and the government, instead of listening to us, is busy finding ways to force

upon us these black laws created by people in air-conditioned rooms'.

Retired Subedar S.P. Singh from Gurdaspur in Punjab said some six farmers were detained when they had attempted to meet President Ram Nath Kovind to return a small batch of medals the previous week. Retired Havaldar Bartar Singh from Patiala alleged that the group of veterans was detained for two whole days, and their phones and other belongings were confiscated. He said, 'I was a soldier earlier, but even before that, I was a labourer and a farmer. We are willing to sacrifice these medals in return for a repeal of the black laws. They kept us in detention for two whole days, thinking that we would go back home, but the first thing we did after being released this morning was to come back here to join the protest'.

Retired Naik Kapil Dev from Haryana said, 'These medals were given not for entertainment but for valour, for coming face to face with death, through sweat and blood and tears, but the jawan is ready to let them go for a better future for the farmer'.

GOVERNMENT CALLOUSNESS

Living in its world far from such realities on the ground and cosying up to the corporates who help it win elections through money and media power, the callousness of the BJP-RSS central government continued unabated. Its leaders tried to defame, discredit, and divide the farmers' movement with no success whatsoever.

Realizing that its defamatory campaign was becoming counter-productive in the face of massively mounting protests, the government tried a new tack. Propping up some of its agents (*dalal*s is a more accurate word) as so-called farmers' organizations, it held negotiations with them. Like a command performance, they duly supported all the three Farm Acts. The RSS-led Bharatiya Kisan Sangh (BKS) and the Swadeshi Jagran Manch (SJM) were also brought in to make noises opposing the farmers' struggle. None of this worked one bit.

In a feeble attempt to draw attention away from the farmers' struggle, on 10 December 2020, Prime Minister Narendra Modi, with much fanfare, laid the foundation stone for the new Parliament building. He used all his usual empty phrases of our 'democratic legacy', 'reflecting India's aspirations', and 'being always accountable to people and the Constitution'.

It was the classic RSS-BJP fascistic forked tongue habit of speaking one thing while doing the exact opposite. Modi spoke of '*atmanirbharta*' (self-reliance) on the one hand while selling off the country to Indian and foreign corporates on the other. He spoke of 'democracy', 'aspirations' and 'accountability to people' on the one hand while letting millions of Indian farmers shiver in the bitter cold for weeks on the borders of the nations' capital on the other.

The peasants, the workers, and the people of India resolved to teach these modern Neros a lesson through this most peaceful, democratic and united resistance India had ever seen.

SIGNIFICANT KERALA ASSEMBLY RESOLUTION

In sharp contrast was the resolution unanimously passed by the Kerala Assembly on 31 December 2020. Kerala Chief Minister Pinarayi Vijayan, moved a resolution in the state assembly against the three farm laws, which was unanimously passed by the house with the ruling LDF, Opposition Congress-led UDF, and even the lone BJP MLA supporting it. Pinarayi Vijayan attacked the BJP-led NDA government at the Centre over the three contentious laws against which farmers are agitating in Delhi. The resolution was moved in a special session that was convened solely to discuss the farmers' struggle and express solidarity with them.

While moving the resolution demanding the immediate scrapping of the new laws, Pinarayi Vijayan said the country, in its history, was witnessing one of the most iconic protests by farmers. 'The central farm laws, passed in Parliament, were not only 'anti-farmer' but also 'pro-corporate,' he alleged. 'Legislative assemblies have the moral responsibility to take a serious view when people have anxieties about certain laws which affect their lives,' he said, adding that agriculture was part of the culture of the country. The Centre had come up with contentious laws when the agriculture sector was facing severe challenges.

Kerala had the distinction of being the first state assembly in India to adopt a unanimous resolution against the black Farm Laws. Some other state assemblies later followed suit.

HOW THE STEEL WAS TEMPERED

On 3 January 2021, Delhi and its environs were lashed by torrential unseasonal rains, which began the previous night. The rain staged a repeat performance on 5 and 6 January. This significantly increased the already bitter cold of January. The plight of lakhs of farmers – children, women, and men – who had laid siege to the capital on all the six borders – Ghazipur, Mewat, Palwal, Singhu, Shahjahanpur, and Tikri – had to be seen to be believed. The people were drenched. Mud and slush abounded. The roads were full of water and dirt.

And yet, the human spirit triumphed over it all. The fire of rage against their class oppressors burnt even more brightly, brushing aside the rain and the cold with contempt. Nothing would shake farmers from their resolve of getting rid of the hated black laws thrust upon them by the most insensitive, authoritarian and crony corporate regime since our country's independence.

This magnificent spectacle rekindled memories of our freedom struggle against British imperialism. The rulers of today were then the boot-lickers of the British.

On the other hand, the fighters of today proudly held aloft the shining legacy of the martyrs in the freedom struggle against the British – like Ashfaqulla Khan, Bagha Jatin, Bhagat Singh, Chandra

Shekhar Azad, Jatin Das, Kartar Singh Sarabha, Khudiram Bose, Ram Prasad Bismil, Roshan Singh, Shivram Rajguru, Sukhdev Thapar, Vishnu Ganesh Pingle, and Udham Singh.

The farmers had combated repression in this struggle. They had overcome defamation. They had fought the pandemic. They would also triumph over nature.

This was how the steel was tempered.

6. THE REPUBLIC DAY TRACTOR PARADES

India had not seen such a sight in its history. On Republic Day, 26 January 2021, lakhs of farmers rode over one lakh tractors on the outskirts of the national capital Delhi. Each tractor proudly held aloft the national flag and the flag of the Kisan organization to which it belonged. It was an unprecedented show of peasant unity that crowned the two month-long SKM-led peaceful struggle.

The most heart-warming aspect of these Kisan Tractor Parades was the love and affection showered on them by the common people in and around Delhi. Thousands of them came out on the streets to welcome the farmers, showered rose petals, and offered sweets, water bottles, and other eatables. This showed strong public support for their cause.

The same picture was replicated in all the states and hundreds of districts. The SKM had given a call for *mahapadavs* and rallies before all the Raj Bhawans (Governors' Mansions) from 23 January – the birth anniversary of Netaji Subhash Chandra Bose – up to 26 January, Republic Day. Lakhs of farmers and workers came out on the streets in their tractors, trollies and other vehicles and held massive rallies at their state and district centres.

AGENT PROVOCATEURS AND POLICE FAN VIOLENCE

The SKM had initially wanted the tractor parade to go along the Outer Ring Road of Delhi. But the police refused and gave alternative routes which avoided central Delhi. Not wanting to complicate matters, SKM leaders agreed, with the clear understanding that the parades must take place – but must take place peacefully. It was decided to begin all the Kisan Tractor Parades from 10 am on 26 January, after the official Republic Day Parade had ended.

In the serious review discussion which took place later in the SKM meeting at Singhu border on the evening of 27 January, it became clear that 99.9 per cent of the protesting farmers in all the borders around Delhi enthusiastically participated in the Kisan Tractor Parades through the designated routes in an entirely peaceful manner.

It was 0.1 per cent of the fringe elements among the protestors who flouted discipline and began their marches between 7 am and 8 am. The police did not stop them, and it was they who entered various parts of Delhi. Some groups went up to the Red Fort and the ITO. Without touching the national flag that flies from the Red Fort, one group hoisted the Sikh religious Nishan Sahib flag from another empty flag pole. This was wrong. Because this was a secular farmers' struggle, not a religious struggle. Police unleashed brutal repression with tear gas shells and lathi charges. One young farmer Navreet Singh was killed when his tractor overturned in the melee. Hundreds of farmers were injured in lathi charges, and their tractors were impounded by the police.

The SKM immediately condemned this unfortunate turn of events in a statement released on the afternoon of 26 January, and another statement issued a few hours later appealed to all farmers to stop their tractor rallies with immediate effect and return to their camps.

WHO WERE THE CULPRITS?

Who were the culprits in this episode? The SKM meeting concluded that there were three main culprits – Punjabi actor Deep Sidhu, an organization called the Kisan Mazdoor Sangharsh Committee (KMSC), and the central government with its Delhi police, all of whom were acting in connivance. Deep Sidhu subsequently died in a car accident recently.

Deep Sidhu was a Punjabi actor who was the election agent of BJP candidate Sunny Deol who contested the 2019 Lok Sabha elections from Gurdaspur. Sidhu's photos with Prime Minister Narendra Modi and Home Minister Amit Shah went viral. From the night of 25 January, he was seen at the main stage of Singhu border instigating young farmers to storm Delhi. In a video clip at the Red Fort, he was seen instigating some youths to put up the Nishan Sahib flag. The same video showed several farmers loudly arguing with him and denouncing him for this act. He was then seen escaping on a motorcycle.

As per a report in the *Indian Express* of 28 January, Deep Sidhu, on 20 January, went on Facebook to livestream several tractors en route from Punjab to Delhi and said, '*Picture toh abhi baaki hai mere dost*.' (My friend, the film is not over yet). On 23 January, he shared a web channel interview in Punjabi, in which he said, 'We can't plan what will happen on 26 January. It would be out of our calculations. It would be unpredictable. It is up to the Almighty what happens on 26 January'. For Sidhu, 'the Almighty' was the Modi regime!

The question must be squarely asked: How is it even possible, given the massive police and Army security around Red Fort, that too on Republic Day, for some youth to hoist any flag at the Red Fort? It could never have happened without 'instructions from the top'. The Nishan Sahib flag was not pulled down immediately and was allowed to flutter for a couple of hours, evidently to oblige the servile 'Godi' media. The clear conspiracy was to drive a religious wedge between Punjab and the rest of the country and disrupt the united farmers' struggle.

The KMSC did not join the protests at Singhu border on 26 November when they began. Its adherents joined two weeks later and were escorted to a separate enclosure away from others by the police themselves. They repeatedly asserted that they would flout the designated route of the tractor parade and would go along the Outer Ring Road straight into Delhi. They also began their march at 8 am, two hours before the designated time. The police did not attempt to stop them, and when the farmers reached Delhi, the police unleashed their repression.

There were many more complaints against the police. At the

Palwal border, although the route decided was 45 km, the police began its lathi charge when the paraders had only covered a distance of 15 km. At the Ghazipur border, the police refused to remove the barricades on the designated route and allowed the fringe elements to take another route.

The conclusion that the BJP government set up these agent provocateurs to defame and discredit the two-month-long peaceful struggle of the peasantry is inescapable. On 22 January, in the eleventh and final round of talks with the SKM, the Union Agriculture Minister Narendra Singh Tomar is reported to have told the farmers' delegation, 'So now you begin your preparations for 26 January. We shall begin ours'. Their 'preparations' were exposed for the world to see. It is gratifying that some sections of the mainstream media and many more sections of the social media exposed this conspiracy of violence by the BJP regime.

SKM COMBATS THE MOST DIFFICULT CHALLENGE

This was undoubtedly one of the most challenging moments in this struggle. I shall never forget the jam-packed SKM meeting at Singhu border held a day later, on 27 January, to plan our counter-offensive. The mood was sombre but determined.

We took five major decisions. First, launch a massive social media and mainstream media campaign targeting the government and its agent provocateurs, with proof of the violence and the Red Fort incident on 26 January. This put the government on the defensive. Second, significantly strengthen our mobilization at all the borders. This was carried out, especially after the widely publicized emotional outburst by SKM leader Rakesh Tikait at the Ghazipur border on 28 January. Third, observe the martyrdom anniversary of Mahatma Gandhi just three days later, on 30 January, in a big way all over the country to reiterate our allegiance to truth and non-violence and also to focus on the RSS's role in his assassination. This call was implemented in thousands of centres nationwide. Fourth, call for a massive countrywide road blockade on 6 February to denounce the government's condemnable repression of farmers in the wake of the 26 January events. This was conducted in over 3000 centres. Fifth, call for a nationwide Rail Roko stir on 18 February. This took place in over 600 centres.

On 27 January, SKM leaders addressed a press conference at Singhu border. While hailing the predominantly peaceful nature of the Kisan Tractor Parades around Delhi and across the country, the SKM completely disassociated itself from the violence indulged in by fringe elements that were in connivance with the BJP central government and its police. It exposed these elements by name and called for their social boycott. It boldly accepted the moral responsibility for what had happened since the 26 January Tractor Parades were an SKM call. In view of these events, it decided to postpone the Farmers' March to Delhi scheduled for 1 February to coincide with the placing of the union budget.

The SKM gave a clarion call all over the country to observe the martyrdom anniversary of Mahatma Gandhi, who was assassinated by an RSS man Nathuram Godse and his accomplices on 30 January 1948, through extensive public meetings and by observing a one day fast for truth, peace and non-violence. Most importantly, it announced that the farmers' struggle would continue and intensify throughout the country until its demands were won.

And then, in February 2021, the SKM began a series of huge Kisan Mahapanchayats in all the frontline states and elsewhere. They were addressed by SKM leaders. They continued unabated till April until the second disastrous Covid wave made them impossible. Lakhs of farmers and workers participated in these Mahapanchayats across the country.

It was this series of collectively decided nationwide actions that turned the tide against the government and back again in favour of the farmers' struggle.

7. DELHI PROTEST SITES TURNED INTO OPEN JAILS

The fascistic state repression unleashed on farmers was unprecedented. In the wake of the BJP-RSS government-sponsored conspiracy of violence on Republic Day, the Modi regime began a massive crackdown on the farmers' struggle. The police turned the three farmers' protest sites at Ghazipur, Singhu, and Tikri into open jails. The *annadatas* of our country were treated like foreign invaders. No other central government in independent India had ever done this near the national capital.

BRUTAL STATE REPRESSION

Brutal state repression began immediately after the government-managed violence at the Red Fort and elsewhere on 26 January. The Delhi police filed several FIRs against hundreds of farmers and their leaders. One hundred twenty-two farmers from Punjab and Haryana were arrested. Sixteen of them were below 20 years of age, while ten were over 60 years of age. The youngest was 18 year-old Deepak from Kaithal in Haryana, and the oldest was 80 year-old Gurmukh Singh from Fatehgarh Sahib district of Punjab. Gurmukh Singh had served loyally in the Indian Army and retired over three decades ago. Over 30 protesters were missing, and habeas corpus petitions were filed to locate them. Several tractors were confiscated, and notices were sent to their owners. Lookout notices were sent to over 60 farmer leaders.

From 27 January, the government began its attacks on the protest camps around Delhi. It first evicted hundreds of farmers from the Palwal border. But the Palwal border protest site was soon fully restored, with thousands of farmers pouring in. The BJP regime then turned its attention to evicting farmers from the Ghazipur border. On 28 January, hundreds of police personnel and RSS-BJP goons started intimidating the farmers there. BKU leader Rakesh Tikait, AIKS senior leader from Uttar Pradesh D.P. Singh, and others held the fort at Ghazipur. It was then that Rakesh Tikait made his now-famous emotional appeal in front of the media. This galvanized the peasantry in UP, Haryana, and elsewhere. This turned the tide, and thousands of peasants from these states started pouring into Ghazipur.

At Shahjahanpur, Singhu, and Tikri borders, the BJP-RSS tried a new tack. They brought in hundreds of their goons who posed as 'locals'. With police support, they started condemning the desecration at the Red Fort, began their stone-throwing attacks on farmers and ordered them to vacate. They were beaten back by the resilient farmers. These incidents had a massive reaction in Punjab, Haryana and Rajasthan, from where again thousands of new farmers started pouring into all these three borders. The notorious RSS-BJP conspiracy to break the unity of the farmers of India on religious grounds by hoisting the Sikh flag at the Red Fort, thus trying to isolate and target the valiant Punjab peasantry, was resoundingly smashed.

On the evening of 31 January, BJP-RSS goons attacked the Kisan dharna at Gwalior in Madhya Pradesh. Many people were injured. The goons who led the attack also tore up photos of Shaheed Bhagat Singh, Dr Babasaheb Ambedkar, and other icons at the venue. The farmers and people of Gwalior hit back, and massive protests began in support of the farmers' struggle there.

Then the BJP-RSS regime wreaked its vengeance on farmers by turning their protest sites into open jails. The protest sites were surrounded by multiple rows of barbed wire, iron spikes, concrete barriers, trenches, razor wire, and huge goods containers. Such a vicious attack was unheard of. Water and electricity connections were cut off. Mobile toilets were removed. Hundreds of local and commando units of the Delhi, UP and Haryana police, topped by a Rapid Action Force, were stationed at all the protest borders. Internet services at all the borders and in several Haryana districts were suspended, creating innumerable difficulties for the people.

Twitter handles of some farmer unions were blocked by the Union Home Ministry.

The formidable iron and cement barricades put up by the police at the Ghazipur, Singhu, and Tikri protest sites around Delhi after 26 January resembled our country's borders with some other foreign country. The *annadatas* of our own country were treated like 'foreign invaders' by this BJP-RSS government. This became the target of nationwide criticism.

PEASANT UNITY TRIUMPHS AFTER GLORIOUS DEFIANCE

The defiant resistance of farmers was only steeled further by the onslaught. Villages upon villages came forward with water tankers, food supplies, and other essentials to sustain the farmers in their struggle against all these formidable odds. Several Gurudwaras and the langars that they were running tirelessly played a truly magnificent role in this struggle.

It is a tribute to this unprecedented farmers' struggle that it not only withstood this multi-fanged state repression but, in fact, increased its defiant resistance. Daily, thousands of new farmers, men, women and even children thronged all the six borders around Delhi. Mahapanchayats of tens of thousands of farmers began to be held in Haryana, Punjab, Madhya Pradesh, Rajasthan, and Uttar Pradesh. Huge meetings were held at the freed toll plazas in Haryana, Punjab and elsewhere. All of them gave clarion calls to strengthen the struggle.

The magnificent farmers' struggle was not only saved but was vastly strengthened by the peasantry all over India acting in unison, transcending the barriers of religion, caste, language, and also gender. Indeed, one of the most distinctive features of the peasant mobilization after 26 January was the massive participation of thousands of women, not only at the protest borders but also in the innumerable Mahapanchayats and toll plaza public meetings.

POLITICAL FIGHTBACK BY THE OPPOSITION

Nearly 20 opposition political parties came together, and their MPs collectively boycotted the President's Address at the beginning of the Budget Session of Parliament on 29 January. This was a remarkable occurrence. They did this to support the valiant farmers' struggle and to condemn the massive repression by the central government and its police.

On 2 February, the opposition demanded a full discussion on the farmers' struggle. When the government refused, there was pandemonium in both Houses and several disruptions, which led to adjournments. This session of Parliament saw many more instances of confrontation of the opposition with the government on the issue of the farmers' struggle.

The Union Budget placed by the Finance Minister on 1 February with its anti-farmer, anti-agriculture, and pro-corporate thrust only served further to fan the flames of the farmers' anger. The SKM, the AIKSCC, and the AIKS attacked the retrograde Budget and called for a concerted nationwide mass campaign against it.

The CPI(M) Central Committee met online on 30-31 January, denounced the central government for its repression of farmers and journalists, and called upon all its units to make every effort to intensify and broaden the peasant struggle further – until it resulted in victory.

Lakhs of electricity employees led by the National Coordination Committee of Electricity Employees and Engineers (NCCOEE), a broad-based united platform of all national federations, observed a one-day total nationwide strike on 3 February. Their major demands were to scrap the Electricity (Amendment) Bill 2020, withdraw the process of privatization of electricity in all states and union territories, and cancel all existing private licenses and franchises in the power sector. This was also one of the important demands of the farmers' struggle. The CTUs, the AIKSCC, and the AIKS fully supported this strike.

The 'Godi' media and RSS-BJP hacks, who had begun triumphantly writing the obituary of the farmers' struggle from 26 January, were thrown on the defensive and had to eat humble pie.

A people united can never be defeated. That was the true lesson of this iconic peasant struggle.

8. CRIMINALIZING AND DEMONIZING DISSENT

ATTACKS ON JOURNALISTS

Along with the attacks on farmers, there were vicious attacks on journalists who covered the farmers' struggle objectively. After 26 January, absolutely false sedition cases and other ridiculous charges were filed against eminent journalists like Mrinal Pande, Rajdeep Sardesai, Siddharth Varadarajan, Zafar Agha, Vinod Jose, and others. Mandeep Punia was arrested at Singhu border on 30 January for no fault of his and thrown into jail.

Such attacks on fearless and independent journalists have shown a sharp increase during the last eight years of the Modi regime. And the protection and promotion of servile and spineless journalists has also shown an exponential increase during the same period.

Deploring the vindictive vendetta of the central government, the Editors Guild of India and the Press Club of India held a public meeting in Delhi, which many journalists attended. Several prominent journalists in this meeting flayed the authoritarian central government and said that the nation was descending into an undeclared emergency.

Another vile act of the BJP-RSS regime was the IT raids on renowned film director Anurag Kashyap and actor Taapsee Pannu, both of whom had supported the farmers' struggle.

ED RAID ON NEWSCLICK

Just a day after the PM's odious speech in Parliament, on 9-10 February 2021, the ED raided the independent news portal NewsClick and the residences of its editor-in-chief Prabir Purkayastha, editor Pranjal Pandey, and others. The raid at Prabir

Purkayastha's residence took 114 hours at a stretch. In a situation where sections of the mainstream media, when asked to bend, actually crawl, NewsClick's only 'crime' was that it had, for the last 12 years since its founding in 2009, been consistently and excellently covering peoples' just and legitimate struggles all over the country, including the current nationwide farmers' struggle.

This was nothing but an attempt of the government to penalize NewsClick for standing firmly with the fighting people. It was another reprehensible assault on freedom of the press, on the freedom of expression and on democracy itself. This repressive conspiracy of the BJP regime was strongly resisted by democratic-minded people all over the country.

WAR ON TWITTER

The BJP-RSS government was thrown on the backfoot when international celebrities like pop star Rihanna, environmental activist Greta Thunberg, lawyer and niece of US vice-president Kamala Harris, Meena Harris, and others tweeted in support of the farmers' struggle in India.

Stung by this, the Ministry of External Affairs (MEA) released a puerile and uncalled for statement, which betrayed its intolerance of criticism. The government then tried to rope in singers, actors, cricketers, etc., to issue counter-tweets. Unfortunately, the servile among them succumbed. But some boldly refused and supported the farmers instead.

This episode showed that the Modi government was being cornered internationally as well.

The BJP-RSS central government pressurized Twitter to deactivate 709 accounts that were critical of the government's handling of the farmers' struggle, on the grounds that they were 'carrying inflammatory and divisive comments'. The government threatened Twitter with the arrest of its top executives in India and a financial penalty.

THE ARREST OF DISHA RAVI AND A SIGNIFICANT BAIL JUDGEMENT

Another episode in this despicable narrative was the arrest by the Delhi police of the 22-year young environmental activist Disha Ravi from Bengaluru on charges of sedition and criminal conspiracy over a 'toolkit' tweeted by climate campaigner Greta Thunberg supporting the farmers' protest on 3 February. The next day, the Delhi police issued non-bailable warrants against two more people in Maharashtra – Nikita Jacob, an advocate and her associate Shantanu Muluk, an engineer, alleging that they were responsible for creating the Google document. The Delhi police, as usual, dragged the Khalistani angle into these actions.

On 23 February, Additional Sessions Judge Dharmender Rana of the Patiala House Court, Delhi, in a significant and courageous judgement considering the times that we live in, granted bail to Disha Ravi, who had been arrested ten days earlier by the notorious Delhi police which is under the direct control of Union Home Minister Amit Shah. Disha Ravi had bravely asserted in the Court that, 'If highlighting the farmers' protest globally is sedition, I am better (off) in jail.'

Some of the memorable passages from Judge Dharmender Rana's 18-page judgement were:

'Citizens are conscience keepers of government in any democratic nation. They cannot be put behind bars simply because they choose to disagree with state policies ....The offence of sedition cannot be invoked to minister to the wounded vanity of government. Difference of opinion, disagreement, divergence, dissent, or for that matter, even disapprobation, are recognized legitimate tools to infuse objectivity in state policies. An aware and assertive citizenry is indisputably a sign of a healthy and vibrant democracy.

'This 5000 year-old civilization of ours has never been averse to ideas from various quarters ....The right to dissent is firmly enshrined under Article 19 of the Constitution of India ....The freedom of speech and expression includes the right to seek a global audience ....

'Creation of a WhatsApp group or being editor of an innocuous toolkit is not an offence ....There is not even an iota of evidence brought to my notice connecting the perpetrators of the violence on 26 January, 2021 with the said PJF (Poetic Justice Foundation) or the applicant/accused ....Considering the scanty and sketchy evidence available on record, I do not find any palpable reasons to breach the general rule of 'Bail' against a 22 year old young lady, with absolutely blemish-free criminal antecedents and having firm roots in the society, and send her to jail.'

India certainly needs many, many more Disha Ravis and Dharmender Ranas, and millions more citizens to openly laud their courage, to halt our march towards a fascistic society.

THE SHOCKING CASES OF NODEEP KAUR AND SHIV KUMAR

After the release of twenty-two year-old climate activist Disha Ravi on bail, twenty-four year-old Nodeep Kaur, a Dalit woman and labour rights activist, was released on bail on 26 February after spending over a month behind bars facing torture by the police. Immediately after her bail, this brave activist of the Mazdoor Adhikar Sanghatan promptly went back to Singhu border to support the farmers' struggle and take up the cause of the workers she had been fighting for before she was arrested on 12 January. She declared that she would go to all the borders of the farmers' struggle, share her harrowing experiences in jail, and appeal to all the people to intensify the struggle. This was courage indeed.

Nodeep Kaur was arrested at Kundli near Singhu border and languished in prison for a month-and-a-half. She reached Singhu border with 2,000 factory workers to support the farmers' struggle. Because of this, she was dismissed from her job at a factory making automobile indicators. According to her sister, Rajveer Kaur,

Nodeep Kaur was thrashed and tortured by the police after her arrest. It is clear that she was incarcerated because of her support for the farmers' and workers' struggles.

One of her comrades working in the same organization, a twenty-four year-old Dalit boy Shiv Kumar, was also arrested on 16 January and thrown behind bars, where he languished for over two months. He was visually impaired. A detailed report in the *Indian Express* published on 25 February gave the gory details of how the police constantly tortured him.

The report begins as follows: 'A report by the Government Medical College and Hospital (GMCH), Chandigarh, submitted to the Punjab and Haryana High Court on Wednesday, has said that a medical examination of Mazdoor Adhikar Sanghatan president Shiv Kumar (24) showed multiple injuries, including at least two fractures on his left hand and right foot, caused by a blunt object/weapon. The injuries are more than two weeks old', says the report.

The same report has even more shocking details, 'In its case history, the report says Kumar alleged that 'the police tied both his feet, laid him on the ground, and hit him on the soles. His second, third and fifth toe nails of the right foot were torn and the nail of the big toe of his left foot became blue. They also hit him on the buttocks with flat sticks, then they tied his hands and stretched his legs. He was made to lie on the ground with both legs straight and a metal pipe was placed on his thigh and rolled over the thighs by two people. They also hit him on both hands and palms and on the back of his head.' It says Kumar alleged that he was 'also not allowed to sleep for three days. The C.I. staff took his statement and asked him to give names, and when he could not do so, they tied him to a chair and poured water on his head.'

Shiv Kumar was finally released on bail on 4 March, a few days after the release of Nodeep Kaur, after spending two months in jail amidst torture at the hands of the Delhi police.

This is the stark reality of the Modi-Shah-led BJP-RSS regime. And this is the treatment that it metes out to those who fight for workers and farmers. And these are most of our Courts, with some honourable exceptions. They let innumerable Nodeep Kaurs and Shiv Kumars remain in custody and be tortured for months, and even years.

Another case related to a Twitter handle called 'Tractor 2 Twitter', which always supported the farmers' movement. The TV channel Aaj Tak slapped a defamation suit against it in the Delhi High Court, demanding two crore rupees in damages without any valid reason. The SKM took up cudgels on behalf of this Twitter handle that young farmers were handling and decided to extend full legal support to them in this case. Apart from that, some other Twitter handles of the constituent organizations in the SKM were suspended. Internet blackouts at the Kisan protest sites were, of course, a regular occurrence.

The common feature in all these vindictive actions was that all the above targets of the government's attacks had courageously supported the farmers' struggle. And that is why their dissent was criminalized and demonized.

These attacks led to sharp reactions all over the country. The SKM, AIKSCC, AIKS, and several other organizations denounced these dastardly attacks on democracy and the freedom of expression. The SKM called for a nationwide protest against all the above attacks on 24 February. This day was observed as Anti-Repression Day to condemn the growing repression of the BJP-RSS central government after 26 January on farmers (122 of whom were arrested), eminent journalists, the vindictive ED raid on NewsClick, the arrest of young climate activist Disha Ravi, and the arrest of young Dalit labour activists Nodeep Kaur, Shiv Kumar, and others.

There was a massive barrage of condemnation of these ham-handed actions in all sections of social media. Youth were especially active in all these protests. Several leading mainstream dailies also editorially deplored the authoritarian trend of the BJP-RSS regime.

PRIME MINISTER'S ODIOUS SPEECH IN PARLIAMENT

Both Houses of Parliament were rocked by the strong support extended to the farmers' struggle by almost all sections of the opposition in the heated discussion on the President's Address, which most of the opposition MPs had earlier boycotted. A team of 15 MPs from several opposition parties, including the Left, went to meet the farmers at the Ghazipur border but were turned back by the police from over 3 km away. All of them protested strongly.

On 8 February, Prime Minister Narendra Modi, while replying to the debate on the President's Address in Parliament, made a particularly odious speech full of lies, insults and invectives not only against the farmers' struggle but also against all forms of democratic dissent. The SKM, AIKSCC, and AIKS immediately condemned the Prime Minister's speech in Parliament.

STRONG CONDEMNATION BY AIKS

The strongly-worded AIKS statement said:

> The AIKS strongly condemns the statement by Prime Minister Narendra Modi who has insulted the protesting farmers as '*Andolan jeevis*' (professional protestors) and '*Par jeevis*' (parasites) and demands its immediate withdrawal and an apology for his derogatory remarks in Parliament.
>
> This insult comes from a 'Corporate jeevi' Prime Minister whose RSS was never a part of the glorious 'andolan' of the people of India against the slavery of British rule. And his talk of 'Foreign Destructive Ideology' (FDI) perfectly fits fascism, which his own RSS has taken from the likes of its mentors, Hitler and Mussolini.
>
> Each farmer as a citizen has the right to protest as per the Constitution of India, and the Prime Minister abusing his power to malign the farmers struggling to protect their

livelihood is highly condemnable. The AIKS appeals to all democratic sections, political parties, and mass and class movements to come forward to condemn this insult of farmers by the PM.

The PM has said that the farmers' organizations are unable to point out the reason for their struggle. This is part of his game plan to malign the farmers struggle. The agrarian crisis is rampant and two farmers are forced to commit suicide every hour in India. The reason is that cultivation is economically unviable due to the lack of remunerative prices and resultant indebtedness. 86% of farm households own less than two hectares of land and they are undergoing severe exploitation in the market and are forced to quit agriculture to join the ranks of migrant workers.

We want to remind the Prime Minister that he and the BJP in its election manifesto of 2014 had promised to implement MSP @C2+50%. Instead of implementing its own promise, the Modi government has surrendered Indian agriculture and the food security of the nation to the corporate lobby. When the PM says that 'MSP was, is, will be', why is he refusing to bring in a law to guarantee the same? Precisely because not even 6 per cent of farmers get the much lower MSP @A2+FL that is declared by the central government.

The farmers are struggling for the demand of legally guaranteed MSP with procurement for all crops across the country. The PM who has violated this promise during the last seven years is solely responsible for the ongoing farmers struggle.

The speech of the PM today in Parliament exposes the compulsions of his government that is under the grip of foreign and domestic corporate capital. The PM rammed through the pro-corporate, anti-farmer and anti-people three Farm Laws in Parliament without consulting a single farmers' organization or a single state government, and even Parliament itself.

The farmers will not step back till all their genuine demands are met, including repeal of the three Farm Acts, legally guaranteed MSP @C2+50%, withdrawal of the Electricity (Amendment) Bill 2020 and dropping of the anti-farmer clauses of the Pollution Ordinance.

AIKS calls upon all its units and all the farmers of India to organize massive protests all over the country against the insult to the farming community by the Prime Minister and prepare for more determined mass struggles across the country.

9. ARBITRARY END OF NEGOTIATIONS

There were eleven rounds of negotiations of farmers' leaders of the SKM with the central government beginning in November 2020. The central government arbitrarily ended them on 22 January 2021. For the next ten months, there were no talks. This was the clearest example of the government's obduracy. The negotiations were fruitless purely because of the government's intransigence. All that it was prepared for were some cosmetic amendments to the Farm Laws.

In the fifth round of negotiations on 5 December, SKM leaders maintained a 25-minute silence during negotiations, refusing to talk until the government agreed to repeal the laws. When the Agriculture and Food Ministers and their aides went into a separate huddle and returned, they were dramatically greeted by the SKM with placards that simply asked – 'Yes or No?'.

On the evening of the 8 December Bharat Bandh, Home Minister Amit Shah suddenly invited an SKM delegation for talks. He refused to repeal the laws but agreed to send a written proposal from the government the next day. The SKM leadership met on the afternoon of 9 December at Singhu border and read out the long proposal that was received from the government. There was nothing new in it. It was just a rehash of the old proposals that the government had made in earlier discussions. It only had a few minor amendments to the APMC and Contract Farming Acts. There were no amendments to the Essential Commodities (Amendment) Act. There was nothing substantial regarding the Electricity Amendment Bill and the Clean Air Ordinance either.

The SKM leadership unanimously decided to reject the government proposals lock, stock and barrel. The anger with the central government among all members was palpable. The discussion then focused on the ways to intensify and broaden the struggle.

The remaining rounds of talks between the central government and the SKM in January 2021 also yielded no result. The SKM was even more resolute in demanding outright repeal of all three Farm Acts. It began one meeting by paying homage to over 55 Kisan martyrs who had lost their lives in the first 40 days of the struggle near Delhi. It took the firm position that discussion on a law to ensure a just MSP and procurement would take place only after the government agreed to repeal the three Farm Laws. There was complete unanimity in the SKM on this stand. Among the 40-odd members of the negotiating team were AIKS general secretary Hannan Mollah and AIKS Punjab general secretary Major Singh Punnewal.

THREE PADAYATRAS CULMINATE ON MARTYRS' DAY

On 26 February, when the Delhi struggle completed three months, the day was observed as Yuva Kisan Divas to felicitate the admirable role of peasant youth in this struggle.

On 27 February, the martyrdom anniversary of Chandrashekhar Azad and the birth anniversary of Sant Ravidas were observed as Worker-Peasant Unity Day to mark the unity of the two basic classes that produce the wealth of our country and against the vicious attacks on them.

On 6 March, to mark the completion of 100 days of the farmers' struggle, lakhs of farmers blocked the Kundli–Manesar–Palwal expressway at all the borders.

On 8 March, to celebrate International Women's Day, thousands of women converged at the Delhi borders, and all the stages were handled by women. The valuable share of women in agriculture, and their participation in the farmers' struggle, were stressed.

On 15 March, the SKM fully supported the CTU's call against the Modi government's drive to privatize public sector assets, against the corporatization of agriculture, and against the massive rise in diesel, petrol and gas prices. These actions were held all over the country.

On 15 and 16 March, lakhs of bank employees struck work. On 17 March (GIC) and 18 March (LIC), lakhs of insurance employees struck work. The SKM supported the strike of both the bank and insurance employees.

On 17 March, the SKM held a meeting with leaders of all trade unions, trader and transporter organizations, and all other mass organizations, to ensure better coordination in the struggle.

On 18-19 March, the AIKS, CITU, and AIAWU held three impressive independent padayatras that began at Bhagat Singh's village Khatkar Kalan in Punjab, Hansi in Haryana, and Mathura in Uttar Pradesh, respectively. They all walked hundreds of kilometres, took public meetings on the way, and culminated at the Singhu, Tikri, and Palwal borders on 23 March, Martyrs' Day. The highlight of the Haryana padayatra was that it was inaugurated by Shaheed Bhagat Singh's niece Gurjeet Kaur, who was herself a part of the farmers' struggle at Singhu border.

On 23 March, to mark the martyrdom anniversary of Shaheed Bhagat Singh, Rajguru, and Sukhdev, both at the Delhi borders and throughout the country, students and youth participated in tens of thousands to take forward the patriotic and revolutionary legacy of Bhagat Singh and his comrades, and to support the farmers' struggle.

SECOND BHARAT BANDH ON 26 MARCH DRAWS MASSIVE RESPONSE

The SKM call for the second Bharat Bandh on 26 March, the day the farmers' struggle completed four months, and for burning the three hated Farm Laws on the day of Holi, 28 March, received massive response all across the country.

The Bharat Bandh call had been given for the following five

demands: Repeal the three Farm Laws; Make law on MSP and procurement; Cancel all police cases against farmers; Roll back the Electricity Bill and the Pollution Bill; and Roll back the price rise of petrol, diesel, and gas.

The Bharat Bandh got a massive response in states like Andhra Pradesh, Bihar, Chhattisgarh, Haryana, Himachal Pradesh, Jharkhand, Karnataka, Madhya Pradesh, Maharashtra, Odisha, Punjab, Rajasthan, Telangana, Uttar Pradesh, Uttarakhand, and elsewhere. The four election-going states of Assam, Kerala, Tamil Nadu, and West Bengal had been exempted from the Bandh.

Markets, mandis, and shops in several cities and towns in most of the above states were closed down for the day. Hundreds of national and state highways were closed down for several hours. Lakhs of farmers and workers, along with women, youth and students, were on the roads appealing to the people to participate in the Bandh, which they did. Anger against the adamant and insensitive BJP regime was palpable everywhere.

Several opposition political parties, central trade unions, agricultural workers' organizations, traders and transporters associations, women, youth and student organizations not only extended full support to the Bandh, but thousands of their activists came on to the roads.

In BJP-ruled states like Gujarat, Karnataka, Uttar Pradesh, and others, several activists of farmers' organizations affiliated to the SKM were arrested. Following the notoriously repressive laws made earlier by the Uttar Pradesh government, the BJP-ruled states of Haryana and Bihar also enacted the most draconian laws to stamp down on all kinds of dissent.

To mark the Holi festival on 28 March, at all the Delhi borders and throughout the country, tens of thousands of farmers and workers made bonfires of all the three black Farm Laws, and along with them, also the four black Labour Codes, and the Electricity and Pollution Bills.

TOUCHING INCIDENTS

On the day that the farmers' struggle completed 100 days on 6 March, Rajbir Singh, a forty-eight year-old farmer from Hisar, Haryana, was found hanging from a tree near the Tikri border. He owned two acres of land, on which he grew rice and wheat. He was survived by his wife and two children. His was the eighth death by suicide at the Delhi borders.

In his suicide note, Rajbir Singh wrote that he was taking this extreme step due to frustration regarding the Farm Laws. He wrote, 'To the government, I am begging you to fulfil a dying person's last wish, which is that the three laws be taken back. Bhagat Singh laid down his life for the country. I am taking my life for my farmer brothers.' The utterly callous and insensitive BJP-RSS government remained unmoved.

Another shocking case was the repression unleashed by the Delhi police, which is directly under the Modi-Shah regime, on Gurmukh Singh, an eighty-two year-old farmer from Fatehgarh Sahib in Punjab, who served for twenty-two years in the Indian Army. He gallantly fought in three wars for India – the Indo-China war of 1962, the Indo-Pakistan war of 1965, and the Bangladesh liberation war of 1971. He retired from the Army in 1984 as Subedar and has been a farmer ever since then.

After the government-sponsored violence in Delhi on 26 January, Gurmukh Singh was beaten and arrested by the police at the Burari ground even though he was not even remotely involved in any violence. He was thrown into jail for 16 days, where he and the other arrested farmers faced hell. He was finally released on bail, but the false case continues.

Gurmukh Singh said, 'I served in the Army for 22 years. I was given a lot of love and respect in the Army. I fought three wars for my country. I have been awarded 10 medals. And now they are calling me a terrorist. I cannot swallow this humiliation. Is this what I have to hear before I die? I am not able to sleep at night these days.' Gurmukh Singh was one among many soldier-farmers who faced such an ordeal.

POLITICAL EVENTS

On 5 March 2021, the Punjab state assembly passed a resolution against the Farm Laws, following the state assembly of Kerala, which was the first to do so on 31 December 2020.

On 8 March, bowing to a petition that got over one lakh signatures from the citizens of Britain, the British Parliament debated the situation in India arising out of the enactment of the three Farm Laws. Most of the MPs were critical of the handling of the protest by the Modi-led BJP regime. International pressure was building up in many countries against the Modi government.

In the Freedom House report on 'Freedom in the World 2021', India, the world's most populous democracy, dropped from 'Free' to 'Partly Free' status for the first time. Apart from many other factors that contributed to this, the severe repression launched by the BJP regime against the farmers' struggle and its supporters was one of the key factors.

On 10 March, a no-confidence motion was moved by Congress MLAs against the Khattar-led BJP-JJP state government of Haryana. Although it was defeated, tens of thousands of farmers in Haryana picketed the houses of BJP and JJP MLAs, demanding that they support the motion.

At this time, significantly, the Governor of Meghalaya, Satya Pal Malik, came out openly to support the farmers' struggle. He said, 'Farmers should not go back empty-handed from Delhi. During my last visit I met both the Prime Minister and the Home Minister and requested them not to use force against farmers. Don't fiddle with farmers ....First they would not go back, and even if they returned, they would not forget the insult for 300 years.'

10. THE MASSIVE MAHAPANCHAYATS

As a sharp reaction to the government-incited violence of 26 January, a series of massive Mahapanchayats began in North Indian states like Haryana, Madhya Pradesh, Punjab, Rajasthan, Uttarakhand, and Uttar Pradesh. Each one was attended by tens of thousands of farmers – from all religions and castes. Thousands of women also participated in these Mahapanchayats. This indicated the impact of the farmers' struggle on loosening long-standing social barriers. But this process needs to continue and be consolidated much further.

From February to April 2021, massive Mahapanchayats were held relentlessly in North India, and they later spread to several other states. They were addressed by SKM leaders, including several leaders of the AIKS. Through them, a considerable churning began in parts of the Hindi heartland against the central government.

Apart from the opposition to the Farm Laws and the demand for a fair MSP law, burning issues like the back-breaking rise in diesel, petrol and cooking gas prices, the four anti-worker Labour Codes, and the privatization drive to sell off the country to domestic and foreign corporates for a song, were also highlighted. These Mahapanchayats immensely helped raise the peasantry's consciousness against the neoliberal, pro-corporate, communal, authoritarian, and fascistic policies of the BJP-RSS-led central and state governments.

HUGE MAHAPANCHAYATS LOOSEN SOCIAL BARRIERS

The other outstanding achievement of these Mahapanchayats was the gradual loosening of caste, religious, and gender barriers and the coming together of people who had traditionally been socially apart. This was evident in thousands of villages. It was an inspiring glimpse of what can happen if peasants and workers come together as a class against a fascistic and communal government and the corporate lobby, which is its bulwark.

One classic example was that of Muzaffarnagar. The 2013 riots and attacks on Muslims incited here by the BJP-RSS had torn peasant unity asunder. The riots had left at least 62 persons dead and had displaced over 50,000 people. Ghulam Mohammad Jaula, an eighty-five year-old highly respected farmer leader who had worked closely with Mahendra Singh Tikait for several years, parted ways after the riots of 2013, along with thousands of Muslim farmers.

On 29 January 2021, a one lakh strong Mahapanchayat was held at Muzaffarnagar. Ghulam Mohammad Jaula addressed it and raised the 2013 riot-related issues amidst pin drop silence.

BKU president Naresh Tikait in his speech, apologized for letting Muslim brothers down in 2013 and also for voting for the BJP and against RLD chief Ajit Singh in the 2019 Lok Sabha elections.

Ghulam Mohammad Jaula then said, 'I have worked with Mahendra Singh Tikait for 27 years. Naresh and Rakesh are like my sons, but they chose the wrong path after 2013. After Naresh apologized and Jayant Choudhary (son of Ajit Singh) touched my feet, we are hoping that the wounds of the riots would heal. Out of one lakh farmers present at this Mahapanchayat, at least 30,000 are Muslims. They felt that they are farmers first and Muslims later.'

This is an excellent example of what the farmers' struggle had done for social cohesiveness.

Ghulam Mohammad Jaula recently passed away on 16 May 2022. He was widely mourned and his remarkable contribution to the peasant movement as a great secular leader was extensively applauded.

Similar examples of caste and gender intermingling in the Mahapanchayats became a remarkable feature. Blue flags of Dalit organizations were seen in most of these rallies. The participation of thousands of women in all of them was a distinctive feature.

MAHAPANCHAYATS IN SOUTH INDIA

The farmers' struggle around Delhi was joined in solidarity by millions of peasants, agricultural labourers and workers throughout the country. Kisan Mazdoor Mahapanchayats of tens of thousands of peasants and workers were held throughout the country, from Kashmir to Kanyakumari, and from Gujarat to Guwahati. Farmers responded in huge numbers to SKM calls.

One massive Mahapanchayat of over 20,000 workers and peasants that I attended was on the sea beach at Visakhapatnam in Andhra Pradesh in April 2021. BKU leaders Rakesh Tikait and Yudhvir Singh, AIAWU general secretary B. Venkat, AIKS Punjab state vice-president Dharampal Singh Seal, and AIKS (Ajoy Bhawan) leader from Punjab Balkaran Singh Brar were also there, along with several important worker-peasant leaders from Andhra Pradesh.

The significance of this rally was its unbending opposition to the move to privatize the massive steel plant in the public sector, Vizag Steel. There are nearly 35,000 workers in this plant. On 27 January 2021, the Modi regime arbitrarily announced that Vizag Steel would be privatized. Assets of Vizag Steel worth Rs 3 lakh crore were to be sold at a pittance of Rs 13,000 crore. The trade unions began a massive and concerted united struggle against this move. It soon became a people's struggle and got the support of all political parties except the BJP. The Visakhapatnam Mahapanchayat fully supported this struggle.

In March 2021, I attended another massive Mahapanchayat of over 15,000 farmers, workers, and fisherfolk held at the southernmost tip of India, on the seashore at Kanyakumari in Tamil Nadu. It bitterly opposed the proposed Adani port that was to be set up there. This would have destroyed the livelihoods of farmers and fisherfolk, and also the environment. Among those who took the lead in organizing it were well-known leaders like M.G. Devasahayam, Thomas Franco, and others. This Mahapanchayat was held a little before the Kanyakumari Parliamentary by-election. The BJP candidate was a strong proponent of the Adani port at Kanyakumari. He was soundly defeated in the election.

SOCIAL BOYCOTT OF BJP LEADERS

After 26 January, the political situation in Western Uttar Pradesh dramatically turned against the BJP. Leaders of the SKM, BKU (Tikait), AIKS and other farmers' organizations, along with leaders of the Rashtriya Lok Dal (RLD), CPI(M), etc., addressed massive Kisan Mahapanchayats in several areas of Western Uttar Pradesh against the Farm Laws and for an MSP Law. They targeted the Modi-Shah-led BJP-RSS regime at the Centre and the Yogi-led regime in the state.

Large boards were put up outside several villages in Western Uttar Pradesh, like earlier in Punjab and Haryana, denying entry to BJP men in those villages. Calls were given for a social boycott of BJP leaders. BJP's Union Minister of State and Muzaffarnagar MP Sanjeev Balyan and several BJP MLAs were driven out by farmers when they tried to enter. In Soram village, Balyan's goons accompanying him clashed with farmers, and the police of the BJP's Yogi regime slapped cases against the farmers. This further incensed the peasants.

The same picture was seen in Haryana throughout the struggle. Huge Kisan Mahapanchayats castigated the BJP-led Manohar Lal Khattar government and also the JJP led by deputy chief minister Dushyant Singh Chautala. Chautala had earlier announced that he would quit the government if the farmers' issues were not resolved by 26 January. Yet he continued to stick on to his post like a leech, to the derision of the peasantry. Hardly any state minister of the Haryana government, including the chief minister and deputy chief minister, was spared from the peaceful black flag demonstrations staged by thousands of farmers all over Haryana.

On 1 April, thousands of farmers from Haryana peacefully

blocked the Hisar airport and the highway leading to it. They prevented deputy chief minister Dushyant Singh Chautala of the JJP from coming out of the airport for over two hours. Eventually, he was forced to fly a distance of just eight kilometres by helicopter to reach the Haryana Agricultural University.

Two days later, on 3 April, chief minister Manohar Lal Khattar of the BJP faced equally massive protests by farmers at Rohtak, where he attended a programme. The police resorted to a savage lathi charge in which an old farmer, along with others, was seriously injured.

Immediately, on 3 and 4 April, thousands of farmers blocked highways and roads in Jind, Hisar and Rohtak districts to condemn the lathi charge on farmers at Rohtak. The BJP-JJP rulers thus got a good taste of the social boycott by the SKM of those forces who supported the Farm Laws.

APRIL ACTIONS BY THE SKM

A Mitti (soil) Satyagraha led jointly by the National Alliance of People's Movements (NAPM) along with several other organizations began from various centres on 12 March – the day when Mahatma Gandhi started the Dandi March in 1930 from the Sabarmati Ashram in Ahmedabad – and ended on 6 April at Dandi in Navsari, where Mahatma Gandhi conducted the Salt Satyagraha against the British rulers.

Traversing hundreds of villages in several states and carrying soil from various historical spots, the Mitti Satyagraha Yatra was welcomed by thousands of people on the way. As expected, it faced numerous obstacles in BJP-RSS-ruled Gujarat. It was welcomed at the Shahjahanpur border on 5 April and then at the Ghazipur, Singhu, and Tikri borders on 5 and 6 April. The soil from all over the country was dedicated to the martyrs of the farmers' struggle.

On 5 April, as per the SKM call, thousands of farmers gheraoed several offices and godowns of the Food Corporation of India (FCI) in different parts of the country, as part of the FCI Bachao Divas, to oppose the Government of India's attempts to dismantle both MSP procurement and the PDS grains distribution. For the last several years, the budget of the FCI has been consistently slashed by the central government. Recently the FCI also changed the rules for the procurement system of crops. The SKM said that this is a grave danger to food security and a serious problem for both food growers and food eaters – that is, for all the people of India.

On 10-11 April, tens of thousands of farmers from the Ghazipur, Singhu, and Tikri borders, led by the SKM, blocked the Kundli-Manesar-Palwal (KMP) Highway and the Kundli-Ghaziabad-Palwal (KGP) Highway at several points for 24 hours. All traffic on this crucial artery that connects the borders of Delhi and is a bypass for all the outer cities, ground to a halt. Huge public meetings were held along with songs and cultural programmes. Thousands of women and youth from Punjab, Haryana, and Uttar Pradesh took an active part. This massive action blew to smithereens the BJP government's propaganda that the farmers' struggle was losing steam.

On 11 April, the birth anniversary of Mahatma Jotirao Phule, one of the earliest champions of the peasantry and radical social justice in our country, was observed at the Delhi borders and across the country. His seminal books include *The Whipcord of the Cultivator* and *Slavery*.

By a happy coincidence, 11 April was also the foundation day of the All India Kisan Sabha (AIKS), the oldest and the largest peasant organization in India. It was formed at its first national conference held at Lucknow in 1936, with the legendary peasant leader Swami Sahajanand Saraswati as its first national president. This day was observed with flag hoisting and other programmes in innumerable village units across India.

On 13 April, the festival of Baisakhi – which also happens to be the day of the notorious Jalianwala Bagh massacre in 1919, when under British orders, well over 1000 of our countrymen were killed in firing at Amritsar – was observed at the Delhi borders and all over the country.

On 14 April, the 130th birth anniversary of Dr Babasaheb Ambedkar was widely observed as th Save Constitution Day. The SKM said, 'Dr Bhimrao Ambedkar was a leader of the dream of freedom for the exploited and oppressed people of the country. He was the architect of the Constitution, on which the RSS-BJP government is making sharp and brutal attacks.'

On 1 May, which is International Labour Day, all programmes at the Delhi borders and all over the country, were dedicated to furthering worker-peasant unity.

On 10 May, the anniversary of the First War of Indian Independence against the hated British rulers was observed by the SKM. On that day in 1857 began, the revolt of the Indian soldiers at Meerut and their march to Delhi began.

Significantly, all the calls given by the SKM during the farmers' struggle coincided with either critical milestones of the freedom struggle, various peasant struggles, the social reform movement, or around working people's unity. They thus sharply demarcated themselves from the RSS-BJP, which had never been a part of any of these struggles but had, in fact, opposed and sabotaged them at every step.

MASSIVE RISE IN FERTILIZER PRICES CONDEMNED

The central government's attacks on the peasantry continued unabated. It rubbed salt into the wounds of farmers by hiking the fertilizer prices more than one-and-a-half times. IFFCO announced the price hike on 7 April. A 50 kg bag of DAP would now cost Rs 1900, as against Rs 1200 last year. A 50 kg bag of NPK-1 would now cost Rs 1775, as against Rs 1175 last year.

Both the SKM and the AIKS immediately denounced the price hike, demanded an immediate rollback and called upon the peasantry to rise in protest against this shocking hike.

The AIKS statement said, 'This hike has happened because the Government has promoted deregulation in the fertilizer sector and companies are fixing farm gate prices without even transferring the benefit of fertilizer subsidies to farmers. Prime Minister Narendra Modi and the BJP Government, rather than helping to double farmers' incomes, are only doubling their woes. This exorbitant hike comes at a time when the farmers have already suffered huge losses due to the unplanned lockdown and the already rising cost of production due to increasing prices of diesel and other agricultural inputs'.

How farmers all over the country are being looted by the government and by the system came out glaringly from yet another fact. It was officially reported that the total pending dues from sugar mills to sugarcane farmers had crossed Rs 22,900 crore for the crushing season that began in October 2020. Of this astronomical amount, nearly 60 per cent, i.e. Rs 13,600 crore, were pending in one state alone. And that state was the BJP-RSS ruled – Uttar Pradesh.

11. BATTLING BOTH COVID AND GOVERNMENT

With the second wave of the Covid pandemic devastating the country in April-May 2021, and the criminally culpable BJP central government under Narendra Modi shamelessly washing its hands off its responsibility for helping the people and the states to combat it, a highly macabre situation arose.

Tens of thousands of helpless people were dying – without hospital beds, without oxygen, without ventilators, without medicines, and also without vaccines. There were reports of serpentine queues for crematoriums and cemeteries all over the country. Thousands of bodies floated in the Ganga river, prompting the Gujarati poetess Parul Khakhar to write her bold and devastating poem – Shav Vahini Ganga (Ganges, the Hearse of Corpses).

The BJP regime, instead of combating this grave situation, plotted to utilize it for stamping out the farmers' struggle. It had already done so in February-March 2020 with the anti-CAA struggle, powerfully symbolized by the extraordinary Shaheen Bagh struggle by women in Delhi. It did that not only by citing Covid but also by engineering the horrific Delhi communal riots in February 2020.

There were several reports in the media that as soon as the state assembly elections of April-May 2021 were over, the central government and the Haryana government had planned to attack the protest sites and evacuate them in the name of 'Operation Clean'. The Union Agriculture Minister and the Haryana chief minister began this drama by appealing to farmers to end their agitation in view of the Covid threat. The government knew well that the protest would have ended long ago, if only it had fulfilled the legitimate demands of the farmers.

The Union Agriculture Minister Narendra Singh Tomar made the ridiculous appeal to farmers to withdraw their struggle due to the renewed Covid pandemic and come for talks. The renewed Covid pandemic did not stop the BJP Government from permitting the massive Kumbh Mela at Haridwar, in which several lakhs gathered, flouting all Covid protocols. There were already reports that thousands who attended the Kumbh Mela had got infected.

Nothing could be more ridiculous than the Agriculture Minister's appeal to farmers to come for talks. It was the central government that broke off all talks with the SKM after 22 January 2021. Not once after that did it concretely invite the SKM for any talks, despite the Prime Minister's jumlebaaz declaration in Parliament that 'the Government is just one phone call away'. The sheer cynicism and callousness of the RSS-BJP government were downright condemnable.

DUAL STRATEGY TO COUNTER BOTH COVID AND GOVERNMENT

The SKM evolved a dual strategy to counter the conspiracy to clean out the farmers' protest sites in the name of the Covid pandemic. It firmly warned the government that farmers would strongly resist any 'Operation Clean' being unleashed.It would counter the government's threat of 'Operation Clean' with 'Operation Shakti'.

On the one hand, from 20-26 April, in a week called 'Resistance Week', all protest sites would make effective arrangements to protect themselves from Covid-19, as given below.

On the other hand, many farmers who had gone back to their villages for the wheat harvesting season were invited to come back to the protest sites as soon as their crop harvesting was done, with *Phir Dilli Chalo* slogan. The powerful BKU (Ekta Ugrahan) called upon its members to reach the Tikri Border from 21 April. The SKM urged all the other organizations to reach out to their members, giving them the *Phir Dilli Chalo* slogan from 24 April. 24 April 2021 marked 150 days of the farmers' struggle.

Effective arrangements were made to protect the protest sites from the Covid pandemic. The pandemic was not new. The spread of the disease was widespread throughout the country, even when the farmers' organizations initiated the protests in June 2020 and later at Delhi's doorsteps from November 2020. Miraculously, there had not been any spread of Covid-19 at the protest sites in the past six months – most independent observers noted this fact. Therefore, there was no basis for the government to point the finger at the farmers' movement.

The following arrangements were made at all the Delhi protest borders to combat Covid-19:

- There was information shared on protective measures to be adopted against Covid-19 at every trolley and tent in the protests.
- Free masks, sanitizers, oxymeters, and thermometres were made available at all protest sites, and there was an intensive drive to promote their use.
- Vaccination camps were started at all protest sites, and protestors above forty-five years of age could get vaccinated here.
- Precautionary arrangements were made to prevent the spread of the disease due to gatherings near the stages and in daily meetings.
- All medical camps were provided with the necessary medicines and equipment to combat Covid-19. Treatment was initiated immediately after any symptoms of Covid were exhibited.
- For Covid-19 protection and treatment, SKM cooperated fully with the local administration.

In stark contrast, the sheer ineffectiveness and hypocrisy of BJP governments in combating Covid-19 was apparent for the whole country to see. The Prime Minister and the Home Minister themselves claimed to have mobilized the largest crowds in the assembly election campaigns during the pandemic. This government thus had no moral right to advise farmers about the pandemic. The SKM condemned the government for spreading fear among the people under the garb of the Covid-19 pandemic, blaming its failures on the general public, imposing fines on them, callously discriminating against state governments led by the opposition parties, and giving corporate houses a free run of super-profits out of vaccines.

The SKM condoled the sad and preventable deaths of thousands of people all over the country due to the lack of oxygen, ventilators, medicines and hospital beds. It rightly put the onus of this colossal national calamity on the BJP-RSS central government. The AIKS released a statement demanding that the central government ensure free and universal vaccination across the country and demanded that the centre stop the super-profits drive of vaccine corporates.

HELPING PEOPLE IN DISTRESS

In the wake of the murderous second wave of the Covid pandemic, which thoroughly exposed the all-around bankruptcy of the criminal Modi-Shah regime across the country and the world, the farmers at the Delhi borders played a stellar role in helping thousands of people in distress. This put in sharp contrast the remarkably sensitive and humanitarian nature of this struggle.

The SKM leaders held a meeting with Haryana government officials, including the police. The farmers insisted, and it was agreed, to remove all barricades on one side of the key national highway at Singhu border, to give free passage to oxygen tankers, ambulances and other emergency services. As per the agreement, farmers on their part immediately cleared one side of the highway. But the police barricades were not removed. A passage was already left at all protest sites from the very beginning of the struggle for all such emergency services.

It needs to be recalled here that on and after 26 November 2020, it was not the farmers who blocked the highways at Ghazipur, Palwal, Singhu, Shahjahanpur, and Tikri. It was the police, under the direction of the BJP central government and its Haryana and Uttar Pradesh state governments, who stopped the farmers and erected huge barricades at all these places.

The notorious BJP and RSS IT cells, in a vain attempt to defend their indefensible central and state governments, began spreading malicious canards that it was the protesting farmers who were stopping oxygen tankers from coming to Delhi. SKM actions blew up all these canards.

Farmers then provided maximum assistance to Covid-affected patients and their families in and around the national capital. They began delivering thousands of food packets to those in need in the villages at all the borders. There were teams of very well qualified doctors helping the farmers' struggle at all borders, and small hospitals were set up. Medical assistance was provided to the local people in the villages surrounding the borders.

ASSISTANCE TO MIGRANT WORKERS

With the severity of the pandemic increasing, thousands of migrant workers in and around Delhi started fleeing to their homes by trains, buses and whatever other transport was available. Migrant workers all over the country had had a most harrowing experience when Modi suddenly declared a national lockdown on 24 March 2020 with just a four-hour notice, without any planning or preparation whatsoever. Lakhs of them had to trudge back hundreds of kilometres to their homes with their wives and children. Many died of hunger and accidents.

The SKM appealed to all migrant workers to come and stay at the protest sites and offered them free food and shelter. Instead of going home to their villages, where anyway no work was available, they were invited to stay here till the situation normalized, after which they could return to their employment sites. The SKM statement said that with this, 'the unity of farmers and workers will be reinforced'. In addition, to help the migrant workers who were going away to their homes, farmers went to railways stations and bus terminals in Delhi and gave them free food packets. It was a touching humanitarian campaign by the *annadatas* of our country and was a stark contrast to the heartlessness of the callous central government.

Farmers at all borders began packing and providing thousands of food packets to help the patients at some hospitals in Delhi. This was taken note of by some sections of the media.

MAY DAY: TOWARDS WORKER-PEASANT UNITY

On 28 April, a joint online meeting of the leaders of the SKM and the CTUs was held. Both these joint platforms cooperated with each other very well ever since their united struggle began on 26 November 2020. In this meeting, the central government's scandalous handling of the Covid situation was condemned, and urgent demands were made. It was decided to strengthen this mutual solidarity and forge united actions on five major issues – Repeal of Farm Laws, Repeal of Labour Codes, Withdrawal of Electricity Bill, Central Law to Guarantee MSP and Procurement, and Opposition to Privatization and Corporatization. A joint statement of the CTUs and SKM with the Covid-related demands and peasant-worker-related demands was released.

On 30 April, an online meeting of the central leadership of the CITU-AIKS-AIAWU was held. It was decided that in this situation of great pain and distress to the people, all three organizations would provide all possible help, support and relief to the Covid-affected people. At the same time, they would together expose the criminal negligence of the BJP government in addressing the severe health crisis and its utilization of the crisis to push through anti-people policies. Though big mobilizations were not possible or advisable due to the pandemic and related lockdowns, and the curfews in different states, the meeting decided that joint efforts would begin to prepare the ground for larger joint mobilizations later.

May Day was enthusiastically celebrated by tens of thousands of peasants and workers at all the Delhi borders and throughout the country as Worker Peasant Unity Day. This was as per the joint call given by the SKM and the CTUs. Thousands of workers joined their peasant brothers and sisters at the Delhi borders, and large public meetings were held to strengthen worker-peasant unity against their common class enemy – the unholy alliance of the BJP-RSS central government and the domestic and foreign corporate lobby.

The criminal culpability of the Modi-Shah regime, which led to the 'genocide' (as the Allahabad High Court itself put it) of thousands of people without oxygen, was denounced in all these May Day public meetings. Also, lakhs of workers and peasants celebrated May Day, maintaining Covid protocol.

Due to the Covid pandemic, the hundreds of enthusiastic Kisan Mahapanchayats that were earlier taking place in several parts of the country naturally had to be curtailed. But these were replaced by online public meetings. For instance, on 26 April, the AIKSCC in Telangana organized a huge online public meeting seen on Facebook by over 50,000 peasants. Leaders of the BKU, AIKS, AIAWU, AIKM, AIKMS and many other organizations addressed it.

On the evening of 8 May, the CITU, AIKS, and AIAWU held a joint nationwide online public meeting on the current burning issues of the people of our country. It flayed the central government for all its sins of omission and commission. The public meeting was widely propagated through posters in Hindi, English and other national languages. Tens of thousands of working people from over 25 states attended the meeting. The speakers were the

General Secretaries of the organizations – B. Venkat (AIAWU), Hannan Mollah (AIKS), and Tapan Sen (CITU).

COMMON STRUGGLE AGAINST COVID AND FARM LAWS

A piece by Rajeev Khanna in *The Citizen* on 27 April accurately pointed out the commonality of the struggle against the Covid pandemic and the Farm Laws. It said, 'Just as common folk have been compelled to run from pillar to post for basic things like hospital admission, oxygen and antiviral drugs, the same will be the case with food grains if the country does not rise against the anti-people Farm Laws.'

12. ELECTORAL DEFEATS OF BJP HAILED

In the first week of May 2021, the farmers' struggle celebrated the defeat of the BJP in the three major state assembly elections of Kerala, Tamil Nadu, and West Bengal, followed closely by the big setbacks to the BJP in the three-tier panchayat elections in Uttar Pradesh. The BJP could retain Assam by the skin of its teeth.

BJP DEFEATS IN KERALA, TAMIL NADU AND WEST BENGAL

Among lakhs of farmers, whose struggle had crossed five months, with over 400 martyrs so far, tremendous anger was building up against the BJP-RSS central government led by Modi and Shah. This was seen not only at the Delhi borders but also in the hundreds of massive Kisan Mahapanchayats across the country that took place from February to April 2021. Calls for a social boycott of BJP leaders were made and implemented in parts of North India.

The SKM gave a public call to punish and defeat the BJP for its anti-farmer policies. The SKM and the AIKSCC sent their leaders to Assam, Kerala, Tamil Nadu, and West Bengal to appeal to the peasantry and the people to vote against the BJP and its allies in the election-bound states.

The defeat of the BJP in the three major states of Kerala, Tamil Nadu, and West Bengal was widely hailed by the farmers in the struggle. In Kerala, the BJP drew a blank, and in Tamil Nadu, it was isolated. The CPI(M)-led LDF was returned to power for the second consecutive time in Kerala, the first state government in the last 44 years to be re-elected. The SKM released a statement welcoming the defeat of the BJP. The mood was jubilant at the Delhi borders and amongst large sections of the working people.

BJP SETBACK IN UTTAR PRADESH PANCHAYATS

The farmers' joy was doubled with the results of the three-tier panchayat elections in Uttar Pradesh, which came two days later. Although these elections in UP are not held on party symbols, it is generally clear which candidate is supported by which political party. The BJP faced a significant setback in most of the districts. Out of the total 3,050 district panchayat wards, it was reported in national dailies that the Samajwadi Party (SP) had won 747, BJP was behind at 666, followed by the Bahujan Samaj Party (BSP) at 322 and Congress at 77.

The 'unkindest cut of all' for the BJP was that it won only 8 out of the 40 district panchayat wards in Ayodhya, 8 out of 33 in Mathura, and 7 out of 40 in Varanasi. It won only 3 out of 25 district panchayat wards in Lucknow, 4 out of 33 in Meerut, 4 out of 19 in Shamli, 4 out of 20 in Baghpat, 8 out of 56 in Bijnor, 11 out of 45 in Muzaffarnagar, and 20 out of 68 in Gorakhpur. The SP was far ahead in many places, and the RLD and BSP in others. Many independents won, whom the BJP eventually purchased. But the message given by the voters of Uttar Pradesh was crystal clear. It is another matter that it could not be consolidated in the assembly elections in February-April 2022.

STINGING SLAP TO BJP IN PUNJAB

Earlier, the week before the nationwide farmers' struggle completed three months on 26 February 2021, the BJP had already begun to pay a heavy political price for its adamancy.

On 17 February, the election results for eight municipal corporations and 109 municipal councils and Nagar Panchayats in Punjab were declared. The BJP was handed down a stinging defeat even by urban voters. Of the total 1815 seats in the 109 municipal bodies, the BJP won only 38 seats. Of the total 350 seats in the eight municipal corporations, it won just 20. But that was not all.

The BJP even found it difficult to get candidates to contest. And many of the BJP candidates who did contest refused to take the BJP symbol. Such was their fear of the people.

The Shiromani Akali Dal (SAD), which had been with the BJP for several decades, but had recently broken with the NDA over the three Farm Laws, nevertheless paid the price. It won 289 seats in the municipal bodies and 33 seats in the municipal corporations. The AAP got 57 and 9 seats, respectively. The biggest gainer was the ruling Congress in the state, which won 1199 and 281 seats, respectively, sweeping 7 of the 8 municipal corporations and most of the other municipal bodies. In fact, independents emerged as the second-largest group after Congress. This situation changed markedly in the state assembly elections in February 2022, with the landslide victory of AAP due to many factors. But the complete isolation of the BJP in Punjab was apparent both times.

In the series of Lok Sabha and Vidhan Sabha by-election results that were declared in early November 2021, the BJP was trounced in Haryana, Himachal Pradesh, and Rajasthan, which were among the frontline states of the farmers' struggle. We shall come to that later.

13. BLACK FLAGS GREET SEVEN YEARS OF THE MODI REGIME

It was a culmination and a catharsis of all the emotions that had welled up in the hearts and the minds of the people of India during the last seven years of this oppressive regime. 26 May 2021 will always be marked in history for the massive participation of millions of people on Black Flag Day at the Delhi borders and throughout the country to denounce the cruel and heartless attitude of the Narendra Modi-led BJP-RSS government towards the ongoing struggle of farmers under the banner of the SKM.

UNPRECEDENTED MASS ACTION

26 May marked the completion of six months of the farmers' struggle, six months after the all India strike by the working class, and seven years of the Modi-led BJP-RSS government, by far the most callous and disastrous that India has had since its independence.

The call for observing Black Flag Day and burning effigies of the Modi Government was observed in tens of thousands of places and millions of households across the country. Thousands of photographs and videos of this action in villages and bastis from every state started flooding the social media sites of the SKM, AIKSCC, AIKS, and other farmers' and workers' organizations since the morning. The rage of the people was particularly reflected in the videos of the effigy burning. Millions of houses, shops, vehicles, tractors and trolleys hoisted black flags of protest. Multiple hashtags in support of the movement trended throughout the day on social media platforms.

That such a massive countrywide action took place despite the deadly second wave of the Covid pandemic was by itself highly significant. In view of the pandemic, the SKM had warned against big centralized mobilizations, with a call to restrict them only to villages and bastis. People everywhere also took great care to maintain all the Covid protocols.

The Black Flag Day call was given by the SKM and was supported by the CTUs, 12 major opposition political parties, including all Left parties, and numerous class and mass organizations. They included AIKS, CITU, AIAWU, AIDWA, DYFI, and SFI. Peasants, agricultural labourers, workers, middle-class employees, women, students, youth, traders, professionals, intellectuals, cultural activists, and journalists participated in the protests with determination. The tremendous response represented the legitimate anger of the people against the Modi regime.

The Black Flag Day was observed at all the Delhi borders at Ghazipur, Mewat, Palwal, Singhu, Shahjahanpur, and Tikri by hoisting black flags on trolleys and tents. Effigies of the Modi government were burnt. The protest sites saw thousands more joining the protests. The sheer determination and tenacity of lakhs of farmers at the borders must be universally hailed. Despite the bitter cold, drenching rain and scorching heat, the farmers had kept up the struggle for six long months and braved severe repression and nasty defamation by the BJP-RSS and its 'Godi' media. Four hundred seventy farmers had by then been martyred in this struggle. But Modi, like Nero, still kept fiddling as India burned, with peacocks for company!

A black flag and effigy burning protest action was held at the AIKS-AIAWU-SFI central office in New Delhi. It was attended by Hannan Mollah, Vijoo Krishnan, P. Krishnaprasad and myself from AIKS; CITU secretary A.R. Sindhu; AIAWU joint secretary Vikram Singh; AIDWA general secretary Mariam Dhawale and joint secretary Asha Sharma, CEC members Maimoona Mollah and Archana Prasad; SFI joint secretary Dhineet Dhenta; and PSM leader Dinesh Abrol, among others. In a press release, the AIKS congratulated the people on the outstanding success of the 26 May struggle.

26 May that year also happened to be Buddha Poornima. Truth, peace and non-violence were emphasized as the fundamental values and principles of the ongoing farmers' movement. Buddha Poornima was also suitably celebrated at the Delhi borders and throughout the country.

TWO CARDINAL ISSUES HIGHLIGHTED

The 26 May nationwide protest was centred on two main issues.

The first was the sheer criminal culpability of the Modi-Shah regime while dealing with the Covid pandemic. As per the official figures of 25 May, the total number of Covid cases in India had crossed 2.72 crores, and the number of Covid-related deaths had crossed 3.11 lakh. But the actual count was estimated by experts to be five to ten times higher. Tens of thousands died in the Covid second wave, many of whom could have been saved. Thousands lost their lives due to the lack of oxygen, ventilators, medicines, and hospital beds. Recently, the World Health Organisation (WHO) came out with an estimate that at least 47 lakh Indians had died in the last two years due to Covid, which was ten times the official figure!

The public health system had almost collapsed due to lack of priority and funds, especially in the rural areas. Private hospitals and black marketeers were fleecing the patients. Instead of providing oxygen, vaccines and medical facilities on a war footing, the Modi regime pursued its obscenely profligate Central Vista project. No one knew what had happened to the opaque and unaccounted PM Cares private fund. The vaccine policy of this government was shamelessly anti-people and pro-corporate. Free and universal vaccination to all was denied. It was only after a public uproar that it was announced much later.

Despite the statewide lockdowns and the consequent colossal

job losses, free rations were declared by the Modi regime for only two months, and these also did not reach the people in several places. It consistently refused to give direct cash transfers to the needy. The nation's economy was in the doldrums. All these issues, along with the Covid-related demands pinpointed in the letter to the PM by 12 opposition parties, were highlighted in these protests.

The second set of vital issues dealt with the Modi government's attack on the working people and our country's wealth to shamelessly pander to the domestic and foreign corporate lobby, represented by the Ambanis and the Adanis. Their profits and wealth grew exponentially during the pandemic, even while millions sank into destitution.

The SKM, after warmly congratulating the people for the great success of this struggle, concluded its press release on 26 May as follows: 'Even though the farmers' agitation has had to continue for six long months so far with many hardships, including the martyrdom of more than 470 farmers, with the protestors prepared to continue for however longer it takes, the determination and resolve of the farmers remains strong and firm. Government of India can choose to remain unwise in stretching this longer without resolving the demands of the farmers, but this would be at its own loss, and at the expense of the BJP's supporter base.'

LARGE NATIONWIDE ACTIONS ON 5/6 JUNE

Within ten days of the massive nationwide actions of 26 May, another set of nationwide actions took place on June 5/6, at the call of the SKM.

5 June 2020 was when the central government first promulgated the three hated Farm Ordinances. It was also on 5 June 1974, at a massive rally in Patna, that the great freedom fighter Jayaprakash Narayan gave his famous call for a 'total revolution'. The nationwide mass movement that began then ended three years later, in March 1977, with the people of India ousting the Indira Gandhi-led

Congress government's authoritarian Emergency regime in the general elections. 5 June also happened to be World Environment Day.

6 June 2017 was when the BJP government of Madhya Pradesh killed six farmers in police firing at Mandsaur. They were in a struggle for remunerative prices and loan waiver.

On 5 June, lakhs of farmers at the Delhi borders and at thousands of places in almost all states made bonfires of the three Farm Acts. This action showed again that the farmers' struggle was by no means restricted to Delhi. Like the JP movement which led to the downfall of the Congress regime, the farmers resolved to work for the downfall of the BJP regime. To mark World Environment Day, farmers planted trees at thousands of places.

On 6 June, farmers across the country paid homage to the Mandsaur martyrs and the martyrs at the Delhi borders, and took a pledge to strengthen the struggle for their rights.

14. VICTORIOUS STRUGGLES IN HARYANA

On 16 May, the BJP's Haryana chief minister Manohar Lal Khattar went to Hisar to inaugurate a Covid centre. He had already earned the ire of the peasantry for his chronic anti-farmer actions and his recent statements accusing the farmers at the Delhi borders of spreading Covid. Thousands of irate farmers from Haryana gathered and began peaceful demonstrations.

The police began a brutal lathi-charge and burst tear gas shells. Hundreds of farmers, including women, were seriously injured. Over 100 farmers were arrested. AIKS leaders who were injured and arrested included Hisar district president Shamsher Nambardar, district secretary Satbir Dhayal, Sube Singh, Shraddhanand Rajli, and others. The valiant farmers gheraoed the office of the IG Police to condemn the repression and demand the release of those arrested.

The state leaders who rushed to the spot and addressed the demonstrators were AIKS state president Phool Singh Sheokand, BKU leader Gurnam Singh Charuni, and others. Immediate road blockades were organized all over the state to denounce police repression. Under all this pressure, all the arrested farmers were released the same evening.

This was certainly not the first farmers' demonstration of its kind in Haryana. As part of the SKM's social boycott of BJP and JJP leaders, several such peaceful protests had disrupted the programmes of BJP chief minister Khattar, JJP deputy chief minister Chautala, and others at Karnal, Rohtak, Jind, and many other centres.

FARMERS WREST VICTORY AT HISAR

On 24 May, Hisar saw a massive show of strength by over 10,000 farmers led by the SKM at Krantiman Park. The government had mobilized over 3,000 police and Rapid Action Force personnel to suppress the protest. But thousands of farmers came in defiance nevertheless. The police could do nothing against such a vast mobilization.

The farmers denounced the brutal police repression, lathi charge and tear-gassing by the BJP-JJP state government in Hisar on 16 May, which led to hundreds of farmers being seriously injured. To add insult to injury, the administration went back on its word and slapped serious criminal cases under Section 307 (attempt to murder) and other IPC sections against over 350 farmers. The farmers' only 'crime' was that they were demonstrating peacefully at a programme in Hisar that chief minister Khattar attended.

On 24 May, the farmers had decided to gherao the Divisional Commissioner's office. But before the gherao began, the SKM delegation was invited for talks. After a marathon bilateral discussion between the administration led by the Divisional Commissioner of Hisar and SKM leaders, it was agreed that all police cases registered as regards the 16 May events and those prior to it will be withdrawn, compensation will be given to the vehicles of farmers that were damaged by the police, and kin of the farmer Ramachandra who died in the 24 May demonstration due to heart attack would be given a job. On behalf of the district administration, the Commissioner also expressed regret for the unfortunate happenings on 16 May. The farmers won a significant victory against the repressive BJP-JJP government in the state.

Prominent SKM leaders who addressed the farmers and took part in the meeting with the administration included Abhimanyu Kohad, Balbir Singh Rajewal, Gurnam Singh Charuni, Inderjit Singh, Jagjit Singh Dallewal, Joginder Singh Ugrahan, Kanwaljit Sandhu, P. Krishnaprasad, Major Singh Punnewal, Phool Singh Sheokand, Rakesh Tikait, Ranjit Raju, Som Vir Sangwan, Sumit, Surendra Singh, Yudhvir Singh, myself, and others. The massive gathering also came down heavily on the anti-people and pro-corporate Modi regime and its disastrous policies.

VICTORIOUS FARMERS SIEGE AT TOHANA

After the big victory registered by the huge meeting at Hisar on 24 May over the BJP-JJP state government and its police, the farmers of Haryana scored another major victory at Tohana on 7 June after laying a massive siege by 3,000 to 5,000 farmers to the police station for three days and nights.

The Haryana state government had been playing a nefarious game to put farmers and police against each other. Towards this end, the police were being misused to strike terror amongst the local youth by arresting them on trumped-up criminal charges. Farmers began their protest against the anti-farmer abuses made on 1 June by JJP MLA Devender Singh Babli. The police arrested three youth activists – Makkhan Singh, Ravi Azad, and Vikas Sisar on totally false charges.

Thousands of farmers stormed and laid constant siege to the Tohana police station, with the demand that the three youth be released and the false criminal cases against them withdrawn. If this was not done, the farmers insisted that all of them should also be arrested. Langars were started at the protest site, and police personnel were also invited to have food.

The protest was led on behalf of the SKM by Gurnam Singh Charuni, Joginder Singh Ugrahan, Inderjit Singh, P. Krishnaprasad, Rakesh Tikait, Yogendra Yadav, Yudhvir Singh, and others. Among others of the AIKS and AIAWU who stayed with the protesters and addressed them were Master Balbir Singh, Miya Singh, Phool Singh Sheokand, Ram Chander Sahnal, Shakuntala Jakhar, Sumit, Vishnu Dutt, and others, while Jagtar Singh was in the panel to conduct the proceedings. The AIKS also mobilized well along with others, with red flags seen everywhere.

Eventually, Babli was forced to tender an apology for his abusive statements. And at the end of the three-day siege, the police were forced to release all the three youth and withdraw the false cases against them. The Tohana victory came on the heels of the Hisar victory, in which false cases were withdrawn against over 350 farmers. Both these victories enthused the farmers not only in Haryana but all over the country.

STRUGGLE AGAINST SEDITION ACT IN SIRSA

Farmer leaders Harcharan Singh and Prahlad Singh and around a hundred other farmers were booked under false cases by Sirsa police under grave charges of sedition, merely because they were protesting against the Haryana Deputy Speaker Ranbir Gangwa on 11 July. SKM strongly condemned the false, frivolous, cooked-up sedition charges and all other charges against farmers under instructions of the anti-farmer BJP Government of Haryana.

Sardar Baldev Singh Sirsa began an indefinite hunger strike against the sedition charges. In the backdrop of the Chief Justice of the Supreme Court expressing disapproval of the use of the colonial era repressive law of sedition in post-independent India, the action of the police was indeed reprehensible. SKM gave all arrested farmers full legal support. Eventually, the sedition charges against the farmers had to be dropped.

TOMAR'S ARROGANT STATEMENT

Union Agriculture Minister Narendra Singh Tomar came out with a highly arrogant statement that the government was prepared to discuss all issues with farmers, except the three Farm Laws. The SKM, AIKSCC, and AIKS immediately condemned this. Tomar himself tasted the farmers' wrath a few days earlier when they stopped his cavalcade and showed black flags at Sheopur in his own parliamentary constituency of Morena in Madhya Pradesh. The demonstration took place even though the leader of the local farmers' struggle Radheshyam Meena and many others were arrested from their homes that morning.

The farmers' struggle was bent on combating all the whims,

fancies, egotism and pro-corporate adamancy of the Modi regime.

A two-time MLA from Amritsar North, and a prominent BJP leader from Punjab, Anil Joshi, publicly said that senior leaders in his party need to shun the 'hath-yog' and show sincerity on the farmers' cause if they wish to survive politically in Punjab. He told a national daily, 'When we have lost municipal elections in Punjab badly due to the farmer's agitation, do you think they will allow us to contest assembly polls? If farmers have dug their heels at the Delhi border for six months, do you think they would budge now? If you cannot put across the issues of those who have shown faith in you, do you still think that you will survive in politics?'

15. 'SAVE AGRICULTURE, SAVE DEMOCRACY' DAY

The 'Save Agriculture, Save Democracy' day on 26 June was widely observed all over India at thousands of places by lakhs of peasants and workers. 26 June marked the 46th anniversary of the imposition of the Emergency in 1975 by the then Congress regime of Indira Gandhi. This year, the people condemned the current undeclared Emergency of the BJP regime of Narendra Modi. The unprecedented farmers' struggle also completed seven months on that day. The day also marked the death anniversary of the legendary peasant leader and founder president of the AIKS, Swami Sahajanand Saraswati, who passed away in 1950.

Before and after 26 June, the SKM also gave other important calls. On 9 June, the martyrdom anniversary of the anti-imperialist tribal peasant leader Birsa Munda and the Sikh warrior Banda Singh Bahadur was widely observed. On 17 June, the martyrdom anniversary of Rani Lakshmibai of Jhansi, who fell while bravely combating the British imperialists during India's first war of independence, was observed. On 24 June, Kabir Jayanti was celebrated to commemorate the great rational and egalitarian saint. To commemorate the memory of the legendary 'Flying Sikh' Milkha Singh, a race was organized at the Tikri border.

The 26 June call by the SKM was supported by the CTUs and several organizations of agricultural workers, women, youth, and students. Its mobilization surpassed the Black Flag Day call for 26 May, when the farmers' struggle had completed six months, and the Modi government had completed seven years of its disastrous rule. The 26 May actions had taken place despite the second deadly Covid wave. This time the situation had eased somewhat.

HUGE COUNTRYWIDE PARTICIPATION

On 26 June, large demonstrations were held outside almost all the Raj Bhawans and copies of the SKM memorandum addressed to the President of India were handed over to the Governors or their representatives. In several BJP-ruled states, rallies were banned, activists were arrested, and the Governors denied meetings.

The anger of the farmers was such that hundreds of rallies and demonstrations were held before several district collectorates, tehsil/block offices and even in villages. This happened in all major states – Delhi, Haryana, Himachal Pradesh, Jammu & Kashmir, Punjab, Madhya Pradesh, Uttarakhand, and Uttar Pradesh, in the north; Andhra Pradesh, Karnataka, Kerala, Tamil Nadu, and Telangana in the south; Assam, Bihar, Jharkhand, Manipur, Odisha, Tripura, and West Bengal in the east; and Gujarat, Maharashtra, and Rajasthan in the west. Hundreds of photographs bore testimony to the success of this struggle.

The mainstream print and electronic media across the country were forced to take note these actions. Social media, of course, propagated them widely.

Two of the largest actions were held that day in Chandigarh. Two massive marches of 7-8 km each were organized to the two Raj Bhawans at Chandigarh. The Punjab march was over 25,000 strong, and the Haryana march was over 15,000 strong. The Punjab march broke barricades and was attacked with lathi charge and water cannons. Anguish letters addressed to the President of India were submitted to both Governors. Several police cases were filed here.

These massive farmers' marches created a tremendous impact not only in Chandigarh but also in Punjab and Haryana and throughout the country.

MOMENTOUS JUDGEMENT

In the context of the SKM's 26 June 'Save Democracy' call, the struggle for democracy got a big boost on 15 June, when a division bench of the Delhi High Court comprising Justices Siddharth

Mridul and Anup J. Bhambhani delivered a momentous judgment granting bail to UAPA-incarcerated anti-CAA student-activists Natasha Narwal, Devangana Kalita, and Asif Iqbal Tanha. These were three of the many youths who were falsely implicated by the powers that be in the Delhi riots case, while the real BJP culprits who incited the riots roamed scot-free.

Among the many memorable and seminal passages in this judgement was the following: 'It appears that in its anxiety to suppress dissent and in the morbid fear that matters may get out of hand, the state has blurred the line between the "right to protest" and "terrorist activity". If such blurring gains traction, democracy would be in peril … Protests against governmental and parliamentary actions are legitimate; and … it is not uncommon for protestors to push the limits permissible in law … Considering, however, that the right to protest is a fundamental right that flows from the constitutionally guaranteed right to assemble peaceably and without arms enshrined in Article 19(1)(b) of our Constitution, surely the right to protest is not outlawed and cannot be termed as a "terrorist act" within the meaning of the UAPA.'

Two days before this judgment, on 13 June, the Left-leaning Bharatiya Kisan Union (Ekta Ugrahan) organized a public meeting at the Tikri Border near Delhi in defence of democratic rights and demanding the release of all those human rights activists, intellectuals, and students who the BJP-RSS central government had vindictively jailed under draconian laws like UAPA, NSA, Sedition Act, and so on. They included the 16 Bhima Koregaon detenus, students of JNU, AMU, Jamia Millia, journalists, filmmakers, and cartoonists critical of the government. Despite heavy rains, hundreds of farmers, both women and men, attended.

The public meeting was presided over by BKU (EU) President Joginder Singh Ugrahan. The main speakers were Prof Jagmohan Singh, nephew of Shaheed Bhagat Singh; myself as AIKS President; noted writers and playwrights Dr Sukhdev Singh Sirsa, Dr Sahib Singh, Navsharan Kaur, Gulzar Pandher, Jaspal Mankhera, N.K.

Jeet; and others. AIKS Finance Secretary P. Krishnaprasad also attended.

All the speakers denounced the fascistic, authoritarian, communal, pro-corporate, and anti-people character of the Modi-Shah government, giving numerous examples of the same. They demanded the immediate release of all those unjustly arrested without trial and sometimes even without charge sheets being served for over three years. They also called for making the 26 June 'Save Agriculture, Save Democracy' nationwide call of the SKM a great success.

On the evening of 24 June, an online countrywide public meeting was organized jointly by CITU, AIKS, and AIAWU. On the evening of 26 June, another online countrywide public meeting was held by the Save Democracy Forum. It was addressed by leaders from all over the country who had faced imprisonment or underground life during the Emergency of 1975-77. While recalling those Emergency days, all of them hit out at the undeclared Emergency of the Modi regime.

KISAN MAHASAMMELAN FOR COMMUNAL HARMONY

On 28 June, under the banner of the SKM, a massive Kisan Mazdoor Bhaichara Mahasammelan was held at the Sunehra border in the Mewat region, on the border of Haryana and Rajasthan. Thousands of peasants – Hindu, Muslim, and Sikh – attended. They included hundreds of women. Mewat region comprises parts of the following districts – Nuh in Haryana, Alwar and Bharatpur in Rajasthan, and Mathura in Uttar Pradesh, and has a sizeable Muslim peasant population.

This Mahasammelan was held in the background of two recent tragedies in this area. A youth named Asif was murdered in a fight between locals. The RSS-BJP and their goons tried to give this a false communal colour and even organized a 'mahapanchayat' to support the culprits to disrupt the ongoing united farmers' struggle. The other incident was the murder of another youth, Junaid, after a brutal beating in a police station. After the protest against it, an FIR was lodged against the communal police, many farmers were arrested, and cases were lodged against them by the BJP-JJP Haryana government.

In this background, this programme was held to cement communal harmony against all provocations. Several SKM leaders addressed the mahasammelan. All the speakers attacked the Modi-Shah-Ambani-Adani nexus, warned against the 'Divide and Rule' policy of the RSS-BJP, hailed the participation of lakhs of working people all over the country in the 26 June protests, and called for a robust secular unity against the real enemies of the peasantry and the country.

FRAUDULENT MSP DECLARATION BY BJP REGIME

The call to 'Save Agriculture' gained even more urgency with the decisions of the central government. On 9 June, the government announced its fraudulent MSP for 14 different crops in the coming Kharif season as per its usual practice. The AIKS immediately released a strongly worded statement, and some extracts are given below:

> The AIKS condemns the Narendra Modi-led BJP Government's betrayal of farmers by announcing Minimum Support Prices (MSP) of Kharif crops for 2021-22 that are neither remunerative nor commensurate to the increased costs of cultivation. It is a mechanical addition of a small amount over last year's MSP without even accounting for the inflation or rise in costs of cultivation due to the BJP government's policies. It has not used the formula of comprehensive cost (C2) plus a profit margin of at least 50 per cent above that for computing MSP. It has continued with the farcical claim of fixing MSP above the paid-out costs plus imputed value of Family Labour (A2+FL).

> This is far below the C2+50 and does not meet the aspirations of the farmers who already are in an acute crisis due to the pandemic and uncontrolled rise in input costs.

Giving concrete crop-wise details of the various calculations, the AIKS statement further said,

> It is necessary to debunk the lies of the BJP Government that the MSPs announced are remunerative. Let alone being remunerative, even these meagre prices are not realisable for a majority of the farmers as there is no assured procurement. Firstly, the huge difference between C2 and A2+FL, even while taking the CACP calculation at face value is to be noted. Secondly, the huge difference in price projection by CACP and by State Agricultural Departments also is glaring ... This is precisely the reason why farmers are demanding correct computation of costs, fixing of MSP as per the C2+50% formula and enacting a law to provide a legal guarantee of the MSP.
>
> AIKS demands that the Narendra Modi-led BJP Government stop cheating the farmers by indulging in this fraudulent exercise and enact a law to assure remunerative prices by rectifying problems in cost calculations. AIKS calls upon all its units to rise in protest and expose this betrayal by the BJP Government.

The SKM statement also condemned the fraudulent MSP declared by the central government.

GOVERNMENT'S SPIN ON PROCUREMENT

The Press Information Bureau (PIB) put out a press release by the Ministry of Consumer Affairs, Food and Public Distribution concerning procurement by government agencies. This was also a well-crafted spin. The procurement of wheat, while it was a record, was only around 39.6 per cent of the total wheat output. In several states, farmers got much lower prices than the MSP. The Modi government made no mention of the looting of farmers by market forces when they were outside the procurement regime coverage.

Only 16.85 per cent of Uttar Pradesh's wheat output was procured, only 8.18 per cent of Bihar's, and only 4.8 per cent of Gujarat's. In other states, it was even less. Farmers from whom the government did not procure and who had to deal with the exploitative markets in these states experienced a loot of over 1000 crore rupees from March to June 2021 (Rabi marketing season 2021-22). And this is in a crop where the government does some procurement, concentrated in a few states. In most other crops, there is no procurement at all. That is precisely why the demand of the farmers' movement for a legally guaranteed MSP for all farmers for all major agricultural commodities assumes urgency and importance.

PROTESTS AGAINST FUEL PRICE HIKES

In response to the call of the SKM, on 8 July, there were protests in thousands of locations across India. In Punjab itself, there were protests in 1800 centres. The protests were against the unjust and unaffordable hikes in fuel prices, affecting the lives of common citizens, including farmers. Petrol and diesel prices crossed Rs 100 per litre, which was higher than the cost of aviation fuel per litre. In 2014, the excise tax was Rs 3.56 for diesel to Rs 9.48 for petrol per litre; in 2021, it went up to Rs 31.80 per litre of diesel and Rs 32.90 for petrol. Sixty-five per cent of the fuel prices being paid by common citizens go to the government as taxes. Similar is the case with cooking gas prices, which increased from Rs 300 per cylinder in 2014 to Rs 1000 per cylinder in 2021. There were 62 hikes in fuel prices in 2021 alone! The Finance Minister informed Parliament that during the three years from 2018 to 2021, the central government had earned a whopping Rs 8.02 lakh crore as fuel taxes!

These were some of the issues focused upon by millions of farmers across the country when they observed the 'Save Agriculture, Save Democracy' day on 26 June.

16. NOAM CHOMSKY APPLAUDS FARMERS' STRUGGLE

On 26 June 2021, the renowned American scholar, linguist, philosopher, and political activist Noam Chomsky lauded the farmers' struggle in India 'as a beacon of hope in dark times'. He applauded the fact that the farmers were fighting not just for themselves but for a society that cared about the rights and welfare of all citizens. He cited evidence of the 'robbery' that the richest have done from ordinary citizens, and pointed to that evidence to argue that the Indian farmers were right in fighting against corporate control of their lives.

Chomsky further said that these corporations are 'tyrannical structures'. 'The protesting farmers should be extremely proud of what they are doing – they are doing the right thing, with courage, with integrity ....For the whole world, this is a model of struggle to carry out the same kind of actions', he said.

Coming from Noam Chomsky, these were enthusing words indeed. They resonated across the world. They were hailed and welcomed by leaders of peoples' struggles in several countries.

The SKM thanked Prof Noam Chomsky for his 'sagacious and energising words of advice and encouragement to the struggle of the farmers of India'. In a letter to him, the SKM noted that his 'principled solidarity and support has bolstered the resolve of farmers' to continue their determined resistance to the onslaught of corporate capture of farming and food security.

REMEMBERING THE SANTHAL REBELLION

30 June was observed as Hul Kranti Diwas in all the morchas. Also known as the Santhal Rebellion, the Hul Kranti was the Santhals' resistance in modern-day Jharkhand against the East

India Company and the usury of the zamindari systems. The Hul Kranti in 1855-56 preceded the First War of Indian Independence in 1857. It was a rebellion mounted by the Santhals, led by Sidhu and Kanhu Murmu, and fought on a uniquely indigenous value system. SKM paid respects to the Adivasis of India, who fought many battles and gave numerous martyrs to keep the country free from exploitation and injustice, and to protect the livelihood resources of communities. They were an inspiration and an integral part of this movement.

UAPA DETENU AKHIL GOGOI RELEASED

Newly elected MLA from Assam and a fighting farmers' leader, Akhil Gogoi, was acquitted of all charges under UAPA and various IPC sections, along with three others, by a Special NIA Court. The Special Court dismissed all charges by NIA, including sedition, and he has now been released from imprisonment. A popular farmer leader of the Krishak Mukti Sangram Samiti (KMSS), he set up peasant cooperatives directly connected to urban consumers to ensure that farmers get a fair price and are not drawn into the clutches of big corporations. He was elected an MLA despite contesting from jail. Such cases clearly show how the authoritarian regime of the BJP-RSS is using draconian laws to harass farmer leaders by implicating them in false cases. SKM welcomed his long-overdue release from jail and acquittal of all charges.

FATHER STAN SWAMY'S INSTITUTIONAL MURDER CONDEMNED

On the other hand, homage was paid on 5 July by the SKM to Father Stan Swamy, hailing him as a dedicated fighter for the rights of the tribal people in Jharkhand. The SKM severely condemned his being implicated falsely in the Bhima Koregaon case, kept in judicial custody, denied proper medical attention and denied bail despite his old age and health problems. The injustice meted out to him by the government, through its investigation and jail authorities, was denounced. He succumbed to injustice from the judicial system also. The AIKS immediately released a strong statement of condemnation of the central government after his institutional murder and demanded that all those responsible be brought to book.

ATTACK BY BJP-RSS GOONS AT GHAZIPUR REPULSED

BJP-RSS goons led by one Amit Valmiki tried to attack the farmers gathered at the Ghazipur border. In fact, with the active connivance of the Uttar Pradesh BJP government and its police, the BJP-RSS goons were able to organize their provocative event close to the protest site in Ghazipur, where farmers had been protesting since December 2020. This was an orchestrated conspiracy, using the infamous dirty tricks that BJP-RSS is notorious for. The goons were driven away by the farmers. But while the police registered the complaint of the BJP goons, the one by the farmers was not registered. In response, protests were organized before many police stations in Uttar Pradesh, demanding that the SKM complaint be registered.

In response to this attack, the SKM organized a Valmiki Kisan Panchayat at the Ghazipur border, initiated by the Valmiki Samaj Sangh, with the participation of Valmiki Kranti Dal, Bharatiya Valmiki Sangh, Delhi Valmiki Chaupal, Chanakyapuri Valmiki Mandir, and others. It was charged that the BJP-RSS forces wanted to divide farmers along caste lines and break their unity. Against this backdrop, all participants of the Panchayat took a firm resolve that they would not allow divisive forces to break the unity of different communities.

SUBTERFUGE BY THE MAHARASHTRA GOVERNMENT

On 6 July, Maharashtra's Maha Vikas Aghadi (MVA) Government moved three bills in the state assembly, almost similar to the three central Farm Laws, with some amendments. Two months were given for the public to give its feedback. While moving these bills in the state assembly, MVA Ministers affirmed that the Union Government has no authority to trample on Agriculture which is a subject that states have Constitutional Authority upon. It was also acknowledged that the Centre has unleashed unacceptable repression on the protesting farmers and that hundreds of farmers have been martyred so far. The inspiring struggle of farmers was saluted. There was also a call to the Union Government to resume talks with protesting farmers again.

While all these statements were welcome, it was also true that amending the central Farm Laws would in no way empower farmers or the farmers' movement. This was seen in the case of amendments moved by the Punjab and Rajasthan governments also. Further, amending laws that the Supreme Court has put under suspension was inexplicable. It was also unjustified that when the farmers' struggle asked for a full repeal of all the three Farm Laws, the Maharashtra government was moving amendments to those very laws. It was clear that the state government was coming under pressure from corporates who would benefit from the laws and perhaps also coming under pressure from the Union Government.

On 29 June, anticipating such developments, farmers' organizations of the state under the AIKSCC banner met the chief minister, deputy chief minister, and other senior MVA leaders to demand that the state government adopt a resolution in the state assembly demanding the repeal of the three central black Farm Laws, as Kerala and some other states had done, and for an MSP guarantee law. They also demanded that any amendments to the Maharashtra APMC Act of 1963 should be undertaken only after running due democratic processes.

The Maharashtra Government's effort to amend the central Farm Laws was strongly criticized by the AIKSCC in a statement released on 8 July. The state government's move was even more deplorable because all three parties of MVA had in the past supported the farmers' movement and its demands. This included a massive mahapadav from 23 to 25 January 2021, in Mumbai's Azad Maidan, in which MVA and other leaders also participated. They had also signed a statement by 12 opposition political parties supporting the farmers' struggle in May 2021.

Eventually, when the central government was forced to repeal the three Farm Laws, the MVA state government was also forced to take back these three bills in December 2021. But this whole unsavoury episode betrayed the class character of the MVA government as well.

17. THE NOVEL FARMERS' PARLIAMENT

From 22 July 2021, the SKM-led parallel Kisan Sansad (Farmers' Parliament) began amidst great determination at Jantar Mantar in New Delhi. It continued till 9 August, on all working days of Parliament. True to its anti-democratic ways, the Delhi Police under Union Home Minister Amit Shah tried to prevent the media and also all sections of the people from coming anywhere near the Kisan Sansad and barricaded them far away from the location where the farmers were holding their Parliament.

A special Mahila Kisan Parliament exclusively by women farmer leaders and volunteers was held on 26 July, the day the farmers' struggle completed eight months, and on 9 August, the anniversary of Quit India Day. Women farmers were at the forefront of this monumental struggle of farmers for their livelihood and future, and the special Kisan Parliaments on these two days highlighted the unique and memorable role that women played.

The Kisan Sansad slammed the BJP-RSS central government led by Narendra Modi on the anti-people and pro-corporate Farm Laws. It took up the issues of a central law to ensure a fair MSP and opposition to the Electricity (Amendment) Bill and the Stubble Burning Bill.

Every day, 200 farmers and their leaders, from various farmers' organizations, came in buses from Singhu border to Jantar Mantar and took part in the Kisan Sansad in a disciplined manner. The AIKS sent five of its representatives from different states every day.

On the first day of the Kisan Sansad, AIKS general secretary Hannan Mollah was elected the Speaker, and Manjeet Singh was elected the Deputy Speaker. Among the other leaders present on the first day were AIKM general secretary Rajaram Singh, BKU (Tikait) national spokesperson Rakesh Tikait, Jai Kisan Andolan president Yogendra Yadav, and others.

Among the AIKS leaders who participated in various sessions of the Kisan Sansad were vice president Amra Ram, finance secretary P. Krishnaprasad, Punjab state secretary Major Singh Punnewal, and Haryana state secretary Sumit.

OPPOSITION MPS TAKE BJP GOVERNMENT TO TASK

The Parliament's Monsoon Session had begun on 19 July. Several opposition MPs took up in Parliament issues that the farmers' movement had been raising. The Halls of Parliament echoed with slogans that went straight from the farmers' movement into Parliament.

The Union Agriculture Minister was greeted by placards that took messages from the farmers' movement. Many MPs moved multiple adjournment motions in Parliament in support of the farmers' movement, but most of them were rejected. Feeling cornered from all sides, the Minister for Agriculture said that the government is 'willing to have talks with farmers, if they come with a proposal'. The proposal was already put on the table by the farmers months ago.

In Parliament, several MPs from the CPI(M), CPI, DMK, LJD, and RJD, held a dharna before the statue of Mahatama Gandhi in the Parliament premises to express solidarity with the farmers' struggle and its demands. The following MPs also visited the Kisan Sansad to express their full support for the struggle – A.M. Arif and V. Sivadasan of the CPI(M), Binoy Viswam of the CPI, Anto Antony and Hibi Eden of the Congress, and E.T. Mohammed Basheer of the IUML.

BJP Minister in the Modi Government, Meenakshi Lekhi, made a condemnable slur in her media remarks by calling farmers '*mawalis*'. SKM strongly condemned this insult heaped on farmers – the *annadaatas* keeping the country alive and sovereign. Her words reflected the derogatory attitude of the BJP government towards the farmers' movement right from the beginning.

RESOLUTION ON APMC BYPASS ACT

The Kisan Sansad passed a unanimous resolution on 23 July at the end of the two-day debate on The Farmers' Produce Trade and Commerce (Promotion and Facilitation) Act, which is in effect the APMC Bypass Act. The Resolution took into account the adverse experience of the operation of the APMC Bypass Act from June 2020 to January 2021 before the Supreme Court suspended its implementation. This includes exploitation and cheating of farmers to the tune of crores of rupees, APMC transactions reducing significantly, and large number of mandis suffering massive losses – pushing them to the verge of closure.

The operative part of the detailed Resolution adopted by the Kisan Sansad was as follows:

> A. The APMC Bypass Act brought in September 2020 should be immediately repealed by Parliament; the Farmers' Parliament repeals this Act, and asks Parliament to do the same.
>
> B. The State governments, in consultation with farmer unions, should strengthen the marketing and storage facilities for farmers, bring improvements in the mandi system to facilitate more transparency, easier participation of more small traders, women farmers and farmers without land pattas, and an end to unfair and anti-competitive practices, to establish more mandis so that every farmer has access to a mandi within 10 km; and the Centre should help in financing such improvements rather than take away the power from the States.

MAHILA KISAN SANSAD OPPOSES ECAA

On 26 July, the farmers' struggle completed eight months. The Kisan Sansad that day was an exclusive all-women Sansad. In the Mahila Kisan Sansad, the debate was around the Essential Commodities Amendments Act (ECAA) 2020. Members who participated in the debate pointed out that these amendments have given legal sanction to hoarding and black marketing by big corporations and others in the food supply chain. They stated that the dark implications of this law were not just on farmers but on consumers everywhere. They pointed out that in the name of export orders, any amount of hoarding can be done by big capital, even in the case of extreme emergencies. The Government has given up its mandate, intent and power to protect the interest of ordinary citizens. Given the gendered roles thrust on women to take care of food security of the household, this law undermines women's ability to provide for food security. When food becomes unaffordable due to this law, we will be forced to eat less. Women will bear the brunt of this law.

Two important resolutions were passed by the Mahila Kisan Sansad, as follows:

> Resolution 1: Even though women contribute quite significantly to our farming, they do not receive the dignity, recognition and status that they ought to. Their labour, hard work, skills, knowledge and their vitality should be taken on board by people's movements and by our society. There should be well-thought-out measures adopted to increase the role and space for women in the Kisan Andolan.
>
> Resolution 2: It is unanimously resolved in this Mahila Kisan Sansad that women be given 33% representation in Parliament and Assemblies on the pattern of local bodies like Panchayats and Municipal Committees. A Constitutional Amendment be made in this regard for giving due representation to women who constitute 50% of the population.

RESOLUTION AGAINST ESSENTIAL COMMODITIES AMENDMENT ACT

On 27 July, the fourth day of the Kisan Sansad, the debate on the Essential Commodities Amendments Act 2020, continued the discussion initiated by the Mahila Kisan Sansad. The Kisan Sansad noted that India's position in the Global Hunger Index is 94th among 107 countries (the following year, it descended even lower to 101st among 116 countries). It noted that the Amendments brought into the 1955 Act have provided legal sanction to hoard and black-market foodstuffs and that this was designed to favour agribusiness companies and big traders at the expense of common consumers and farmers.

The Kisan Sansad further noted that the de-regulation of food supply chains would lead to domination by big corporate and global food processing and marketing companies. The Sansad took serious cognizance of the need to ensure food security for everyone at affordable prices, whereas the Amendments to the Act allow the government to impose stock limits only in the case of 'extraordinary price rise'. Worse, many entities need not comply with stock limits even in the case of emergencies due to the exceptions provided even in the severely limited powers of regulation with the government.

The operative part of the detailed resolution adopted by the Kisan Sansad was as follows:

A. The Essential Commodities Amendment Act 2020 should be immediately repealed by Parliament; the Farmers' Parliament repeals this Act, and asks Parliament to do the same.

B. The State governments, in consultation with farmers' unions, should strengthen the marketing, transportation, storage facilities and food processing for crops; bring improvements in the food delivery system to ensure basic food and nutrition security to all people.

C. The Government of India should frame a policy and ensure establishment of such basic facilities and infrastructure that will ensure that farmers and their families, not corporates and

MNCs, earn from the food production, storage, processing and marketing.'

RESOLUTION AGAINST CONTRACT FARMING ACT

The SKM-organized parallel Kisan Sansad in Delhi entered the third week, with 200 farmers from different organizations participating daily. Rains lashed the protest sites. But in the Kisan Sansad at Jantar Mantar, proceedings were not allowed to be disrupted by the rain and even floods, with members keeping to the timeline and discussing the topics in detail. Lunch was eaten happily, squatting on wet pavements at this Sansad.

Members who participated in the debate shared their own personal experiences with contract farming. Experiences included rejection of produce by companies under one garb or the other after an entire season's toil by the farmer. They talked about how the central law facilitates corporate farming and resource-grabbing. The potential threat to food security and to peasants' land ownership from contract farming was highlighted, in addition to environmental degradation. Members also pointed out the cruel joke on farmers, and the irony in the very name of the legislation ('price assurance'), when it was anything but that.

On 29 July, after a two-day debate, the Kisan Sansad unanimously rejected The Farmers' (Empowerment and Protection) Agreement of Price Assurance and Farm Services Act 2020 as unconstitutional, anti-farmer, and pro-corporate, and declared that the Act stands repealed. It was resolved that the Act is meant for resource grabbing by corporates from farmers, and was, in fact, brought in to promote corporate farming. Various sections of this legislation clearly showed that it was meant to exempt corporations from the regulatory purview of multiple laws, whereas there were no protective provisions worth speaking about for the farmer who entered into contract farming. The provision in the law banning aggrieved farmers from taking recourse to the Courts, came in for the heaviest criticism.

The operative part of the detailed resolution adopted by the Kisan Sansad was as follows:

A. The Farmers Agreement on Price Assurance and Farm Services Act 2020 (No 20 of 2020) should be immediately repealed by Parliament; the Farmers' Parliament repeals this Act, and asks Parliament to do the same.

B. Full protection is offered to uphold farmers' interests (economic viability, environmental sustainability and social equity) in all marketing options that exist for them such that any contract farming option is only based on prior informed consent, on par with other options available to a farmer and not on coercion. Further, strong regulation should be put in place at the state level which protects the small farmers from predatory contract farming, which fixes clear accountability and liability on the companies which enter into contract farming arrangements, which stipulates that the companies should provide at least the Minimum Support Price to the farmers, which ensures access to justice for the farmers and speedy resolution of cases where farmers face losses due to exploitative practices of the companies, and which removes any provisions which enable corporate takeover of the farmers' lands.

RESOLUTION AGAINST ELECTRICITY AMENDMENT BILL

On 30 July and 2 August, in the Kisan Sansad, the debate and proceedings were on the Electricity Amendment Bill. This was listed for introduction in the monsoon session of Parliament. The Kisan Sansad expressed shock and dismay at the government reneging on its commitment on 30 December 2020 to farmer leaders that the Electricity Amendment Bill 2020 would be withdrawn. The Kisan

Sansad concluded that the Electricity Amendment Bill, like other legislations being thrust by the Modi government on farmers and other common citizens in an unconstitutional and undemocratic way, was meant basically to facilitate the entry and profitable operations of corporations into the distribution of electricity. The Bill sought to thrust a national tariff policy, violating the authority of state governments in determining their policies.

The Bill would put an end to cross-subsidies, and ensure that commercial entities and industries benefit from lower costs. In the name of DBT of subsidies, this legislation would translate the policy plans of ending subsidies in this sector into reality.

The operative part of the detailed resolution adopted by the Kisan Sansad was as follows:

> A. The Electricity Amendment Bill 2020 or 2021 is withdrawn immediately;
> B. The Government of India is directed not to table this Bill or any other Bill containing similar provisions in this or subsequent sessions of Parliament;
> C. Electricity being a basic resource for rural production and processing including by farmers, cottage industries, for health, education and other civic services, the policy should be to provide free, high quality, regular supply of electricity, to enable rural people and farmers to benefit from the same.

RESOLUTION AGAINST STUBBLE BURNING BILL

In the Lok Sabha on 3 August, The Commission for Air Quality Management in National Capital Region and Adjoining Areas Bill, 2021 was introduced amidst continued protests by Opposition MPs on various issues, including the black Farm Laws. While Section 14 related to Penalties says that 'the provisions of this section shall not apply to any farmer for causing air pollution by stubble burning or mismanagement of agricultural residue', there is a new provision introduced insidiously by the government. This new Section 15, titled misleadingly as 'Environmental Compensation', says that 'the Commission may impose and collect Environmental Compensation from farmers causing air pollution by stubble burning, at such rate and in such manner, as may be prescribed'. The government was warned against playing games with protesting farmers and reneging on commitments already made.

The operative part of the detailed resolution adopted by the Kisan Sansad was as follows:

A. The Kisan Sansad deletes the penal provisions on farmers in the 'Commission on Air Quality Management in NCR and Adjoining Areas' Bill 2021, and directs Parliament to do so.
B. Calls upon the Union Government to make all necessary financial arrangements to incentivize farmers to take up sustainable practices, and for state governments to sincerely address the stubble burning issue. This should include consultative and participatory processes with farmers on all aspects including scientific studies.

RESOLUTION FOR MSP LEGAL GUARANTEE

On 4 and 5 August, the Kisan Sansad discussed the current situation concerning the cost of production calculations by the Government of India, wherein several costs were being suppressed. The Kisan Sansad condemned the fact that the Modi government was using wrong cost concepts for the MSP declaration in a deceitful manner. Instead of using a C2+50% formula, the government is using the A2+FL (Family Labour) formula, flouting the recommendation of the Swaminathan Commission. Many agricultural commodities do not have any MSP declared, while the MSP that is declared is meaningless without mechanisms for guaranteeing such an MSP to every farmer through procurement.

The Kisan Sansad passed a resolution directing the Government of India to immediately table a Bill that will fully address the current injustice in terms of cost calculations, MSP formula and guaranteed MSP operationalization. Such a statute should cover all agricultural commodities and all farmers. It also asked for the implementation of the many progressive recommendations of the Swaminathan Commission.

The operative part of the detailed resolution adopted by the Kisan Sansad was as follows:

A. The Government of India is directed to introduce a Bill that incorporates the following essential elements immediately and the Indian Parliament is directed to pass the same:-
- which will confer remunerative price of at least 50% over the comprehensive cost of production C2 as recommended by the National Commission on Farmers, plus some agricultural commodities getting MSP at more than C2+50% to address the skewed cropping patterns;
- which will also address cost components that are being miscalculated and suppressed at this point of time, as well as improve the surveys which arrive at cost estimations as per the Ramesh Chand Committee report;
- that such a statute incorporate institutional architecture required for making remunerative MSP a reality for all farmers;

B. The Government of India and state governments where required, are directed to implement immediately progressive recommendations in the National Commission on Farmers reports (Swaminathan Commission) related to operationalization of the definition of 'Farmer', prevention of acquisition of agricultural land, on provision of pensions to all farmers, on providing universal, effective and adequate crop insurance and disaster compensation to all farmers for all kinds of risks etc.

KISAN SANSAD ADOPTS NO-CONFIDENCE MOTION AGAINST MODI REGIME

On its 13th and concluding day on 9 August, the all-women Kisan Parliament passed a unanimous resolution expressing no-confidence in the BJP-led Modi government. This special session gave a clarion call to the people to oust the corporates from agriculture (Corporates Kheti Chhodo) and asked the BJP government to quit (Modi Sarkar Gaddi Chhodo) as it has failed the people by pursuing anti-farmer, anti-worker, anti-people, pro-corporate, authoritarian, and communal policies ever since it came to power in 2014.

The no-confidence motion was tabled in the House on 6 August, and it was debated for two days. It was based on the fact that the farmers' demands were not being met, despite more than eight months of peaceful protests by lakhs of farmers across the country. Speakers launched a scathing attack on the BJP-RSS government, which had lost the confidence of the people. During the pandemic, it bulldozed the anti-farmer and anti-worker laws through Parliament. As many as 90 women speakers expressed their views on the motion.

The no-confidence motion said that the Modi government had created a hoax of doubling farmers' incomes and had done nothing concrete towards this. The motion also mentioned that the BJP and the Prime Minister have reneged on their MSP-related promises time and again, including making a C2+50% MSP a reality for all farmers. The government had also cheated farmers on the much-hyped Pradhan Mantri Fasal Bima Yojana (PMFBY), where government expenditure increased, farmers' coverage decreased, and corporate super-profits escalated. On the import-export front, India's exports declined while imports increased. Government support to farmers during natural calamities was a massive failure.

Several issues of grave concern to ordinary citizens were also raised during the debate on the no-confidence motion. These included an unaffordable and unjustified hike in fuel prices affecting all ordinary citizens of the country, the collapse of an under-invested and unprepared health care system in the Covid pandemic, putting our democracy into jeopardy by unconscionable spying on citizens and elected leaders by the government, serious human rights violations in the name of sedition, UAPA, NSA, and other archaic laws and false charges on defenders of democracy, foisting anti-worker laws to protect big capital, and several other anti-farmer measures by the government. While participating in the debate, Kisan Parliamentarians raised numerous issues concerning their livelihoods and violation of democratic values and basic human rights.

The Mahila Kisan Sansad on 9 August also deliberated on the issues of women farmers. 9 August was International Indigenous People's Day too. Adivasis were an important group of farmers, and the MSP legal guarantee demand sought to secure a guaranteed MSP for forest produce and other commodities. Adivasis were also waging struggles to uphold their rights over various natural resources, including land and forests. The Kisan Sansad fully supported all their struggles.

The House resolved to adjourn the Kisan Parliament sine die in view of the preparations for the next SKM programmes, i.e. 15 August Independence Day to be celebrated as Kisan Mazdoor Azaadi Sangram Divas and Mission UP-Uttarakhand.

The House also passed a resolution hailing the performance of our players in the Tokyo Olympic Games by winning Gold, Silver and Bronze Medals for the country.

OPPOSITION MPS VISIT KISAN SANSAD

On 6 August, MPs of different Opposition political parties visited the Kisan Sansad. They watched and listened to the proceedings of the Kisan Sansad in a specially arranged Visitors'

Gallery. These MPs said in their media bytes that they were extending their full support to the protesting farmers on their demands. MPs belonging to various parties like the Congress, CPI(M), CPI, DMK, IUML, RJD, RSP, Shiv Sena, TMC, etc., visited the Kisan Sansad. The Speaker of the Kisan Sansad thanked the Opposition MPs of India's Parliament for their support.

On the other hand, the Kisan Sansad also noted that parties like the AIADMK, BJD, JD(U), TRS, TDP, and YSRCP have been participating against the interests of farmers in Parliamentary debates on various Bills. SKM warned them against their anti-people positions.

AUTHORITARIAN BJP STANCE IN PARLIAMENT CONDEMNED

While the Kisan Sansad continued in its disciplined manner of detailed deliberations and debates, the Parliament of India presented a contrasting picture, but with the theme of the farmers' struggle reflected there too. The Question Hour reflected the concerns of farmers. Placards were carried into the House and displayed. There were repeated adjournments.

A delegation of leaders from various political parties met with President Shri Ram Nath Kovind, seeking his intervention to form a joint parliamentary panel to investigate hundreds of deaths during the farmers' struggle. These parties contested the Government of India's claim that it has no record of any farmer deaths in the ongoing movement and demanded a Joint Parliamentary Committee probe into the deaths.

It was reported that Parliament functioned for only 18 out of 107 hours because the opposition's legitimate demand that pressing issues of common citizens and issues related to the protection of Indian democracy were not met, despite numerous adjournment motion notices put in. This was clearly the case of an egoistic and adamant BJP-RSS government continuing its undemocratic functioning, squandering crores of rupees by not listening to the opposition and not allowing them to raise essential matters. Twelve bills were passed in this session of the Parliament without any discussion.

The bulldozing of the parliamentary procedure showed the authoritarian trends of the government.

18. THE 9 AUGUST WORKER-PEASANT STRUGGLE

9 August 2021 was a truly memorable day. The vibrancy and determination of the Left movement were on full display throughout India. Lakhs of people were mobilized by the Left class and mass fronts AIKS, CITU, AIAWU, AIDWA, DYFI, SFI in hundreds of districts in 25 states across India on the slogan of 'Save India' from Corporate Communalism, symbolized by the bankrupt BJP-RSS regime and its unholy alliance with the rapacious corporate lobby. Seventy-nine years ago, on the same day in 1942, the country had reverberated on the Quit India slogan given by Mahatma Gandhi against the hated British imperialist rulers.

The massive action evoked memories of the 9 August nationwide Jail Bharo struggle three years ago in 2018, at the joint call of the CITU-AIKS-AIAWU. Over five lakh had then courted arrest. This was immediately followed by the massive two-lakh strong Delhi rally to Parliament by these three class organizations on 5 September 2018. Red flags dominated the capital that day.

From Delhi, Haryana, Himachal Pradesh, Jammu and Kashmir, Punjab, Uttarakhand, and Uttar Pradesh to the north; to Andhra Pradesh, Karnataka, Kerala, Tamil Nadu, and Telangana to the south; from Assam, Bihar, Jharkhand, Odisha, Tripura, and West Bengal to the east; to Gujarat, Maharashtra, and Rajasthan to the west; and Madhya Pradesh and Chhattisgarh in the centre; there were huge protest actions everywhere. They took myriad forms of Jail Bharo, Chakka Jaam, gherao of government offices, rallies, demonstrations, and dharnas.

Along with workers, peasants and agricultural labourers, women, youth and students hailing from all religions, castes, and creeds thronged these massive protests. They squarely attacked the abysmal failure of the corporate-backed fascistic and communal Modi government on all fronts. Thousands of photos of the 9 August actions poured in from all over the country.

MAJOR DEMANDS OF STRUGGLE

The major demands of this struggle were the repeal of the three anti-people Farm Laws and the four anti-worker Labour Codes; withdrawal of the Electricity Amendment Bill; central law to guarantee procurement at an MSP of C2+50% for all crops; end to privatization and disinvestment of the public sector and selling off the country to corporates; immediate slashing of the massive and continuing price hikes of diesel, petrol, gas, cooking oil and all other essential commodities; increase the budget allocation on MGNREGA to ensure minimum 200 days work at Rs 600 per day; enact the Urban Employment Guarantee Scheme; compensate job and wage losses during the pandemic; register all migrant and unorganized sector workers; address loss of jobs and livelihood issues and create more jobs; fill up all vacancies in government and public sector immediately; ensure minimum wages and social security and pension to all workers; cash transfer of Rs 7500 per month for all non income tax paying families; 10 kg free food grains per person per month for the entire period of the pandemic; ensure immediate free and universal vaccination to all with priority to frontline workers; ramp up vaccine production and bring the distribution under government regulation to ensure universal free vaccination within a definite time frame; scrap the pro-corporate vaccination policy; allocate 6 per cent of GDP for health sector; strengthen the public health system and the health infrastructure to ensure adequate hospital beds, oxygen and other medical facilities to meet the Covid surge; strengthen public health infrastructure including recruiting the necessary health personnel; ensure that non-Covid patients get effective treatment in government hospitals; ensure availability of protective gear, equipments, wage rise etc for all health and frontline workers and those engaged in pandemic-management work including ASHAs and Anganwadi employees along with comprehensive insurance coverage for them all; withdraw draconian EDSO; and scrap new education policy and ensure good education to all students in the pandemic.

SKM DECLARES MISSION UP-UTTARAKHAND

The SKM launched Mission Uttar Pradesh and Uttarakhand on 26 July at a press conference in Lucknow. It was announced that the Mission would formally begin with a massive rally in Muzaffarnagar on 5 September 2021. It was also announced that the current farmers' movement would be taken to every village in the two states to strengthen it the way it has happened in Punjab and Haryana. Through this, corporate control of our food and farming systems will also be challenged from all corners of these states. In this Mission, the anti-farmer BJP and its allies would be resisted and boycotted everywhere, like their leaders were facing boycotts and protests in Punjab and Haryana.

The venerated land of Swami Sahajanand Saraswati, Choudhary Charan Singh, and Choudhary Mahendra Singh Tikait would now take up the fight of protecting India's farming and farmers from corporates and their political brokers. The SKM called upon farmers' unions and other progressive forces to join hands. Protests would be organized at Ambani and Adani entities in the two states. For giving shape and effect to this Mission, there would be meetings, dialogues, yatras, and rallies organized throughout the two states.

The choice of Muzaffarnagar for the opening rally of the SKM was significant. For it was Muzaffarnagar in 2013 that saw bloody communal riots that were instigated by the BJP-RSS and unfortunately supported by some other forces who should have known better. These riots created the communal polarization in North India that swept the BJP to power in 2014 at the centre and in 2017 in the state. However, the strength of the farmers' struggle and the Covid-related and other numerous crimes of the Modi-Yogi-led BJP governments were changing the picture in Uttar

Pradesh. The farmers' class struggle was once again cementing communal harmony.

On 31 July, the martyrdom day of Shaheed Udham Singh was marked as Anti-Imperialist Day. In several morchas, revolutionary songs provided inspiration to the protestors, and speakers highlighted the life, struggle, and sacrifice of Shaheed Udham Singh the independence struggle, and the struggle against imperialism and human plunder.

SUPREME COURT RECOGNIZES FARMERS' RIGHT TO PROTEST

In the Supreme Court's comments in the hearing of a two-judge bench on a PIL, the Court recognized the farmers' right to protest peacefully. SKM pointed out that the blockades were not created by the farmers, but by the police and administration of multiple state governments and the Delhi Police under the control of the Government of India. Farmers were not living on the streets for nearly nine months out of their wish and desire, but because governments put up blockades when they wished to go to the heart of Delhi to get their grievances heard.

It was the government that was not willing to resolve the stalemate. The Supreme Court said that the Union Government should take early steps to resolve the matter. This resolution could only come from resuming dialogue with the SKM and fulfilling the farmers' legitimate demands. Nearly 600 farmers have been martyred in this agitation so far, but the BJP-RSS government was unmoved by the hardships of the protestors and was not even willing to acknowledge the farmers' deaths.

19. TIRANGA RALLIES COUNTER LIES AND DECEITS

While Prime Minister Narendra Modi was rolling out more than his usual quota of lies, deceits, and *jumlas* in his speech at the Red Fort, India's 75th Independence Day, 15 August 2021, was marked by lakhs of farmers and workers organizing huge Tiranga Yatras on Kisan Mazdoor Azaadi Sangram Diwas all over India, including at the protest sites at Delhi's borders. Tiranga is the tricolour national flag of India.

Never before in independent India, except when India gained independence in 1947, was the day marked so visibly and with so much fervour. Thousands of vehicles of farmers were taken out in Tiranga Yatras in different places, spanning hundreds of kilometres. In agricultural fields and the chowks of urban centres, the Tiranga was held high, with farmers and other ordinary citizens taking the lead, even as they highlighted issues that need redressal for true freedom to be experienced by all citizens, especially by the most marginalized.

Reports poured in from different locations about the various ways in which the day was marked by farmers and workers. Women farmers took the lead in different places in Haryana, Punjab, and elsewhere. There were special events to mark the day at the various morchas of the farmers' struggle, including Ghazipur, Mewat, Palwal, Shahjahanpur, Singhu, and Tikri. The Azaadi Sangram Diwas was also marked at different toll plazas, which had become pucca morchas of protesting farmers over the past several months. As expected, the Uttar Pradesh police did not allow the Tiranga Yatras of farmers in some locations to proceed.

AIKS LAMBASTS PM'S SPEECH

The Prime Minister's Independence Day Speech refused to mention the farmers' movement, and instead made hollow claims yet again about policies favouring small and marginal farmers of the country. There was a deafening silence on his earlier claims and commitments of 'doubling farmers' incomes'. The AIKS, in a press note released on Independence Day, condemned the lies and deceits resorted to by the Prime Minister and resolved to intensify the countrywide campaign to expose this callous BJP government.

The AIKS statement said,

> Prime Minister Narendra Modi who refused to speak on the plight of the farmers in Parliament or to resolve issues raised by them, used the solemn occasion of Independence Day to hoodwink the nation and falsely portray that the BJP Government has been doing a lot for farmers. Farmers have been protesting on the borders of Delhi and across the country for more than nine months and over 600 farmers have become martyrs in the struggle, but the Prime Minister adamantly pursues the policies promoting corporate profiteering. If he was really concerned about small farmers he should have announced the decision to repeal the three Farm Acts, amendments to Electricity Act and announce a law to make MSP a legal right.
>
> The bitter truth is that in the last seven years of Narendra Modi's rule farmers' incomes have dwindled instead of his claim of doubling incomes, and farm suicides have crossed a lakh. The Pradhan Mantri Fasal Bima Yojana (PMFBY) which he highlighted as helping small farmers has actually become a monumental failure. Lakhs of farmers' claims are not being settled although premium is paid by them as well as by state and central governments. Many States including Andhra Pradesh, Bihar, Punjab, Telangana, West Bengal and Modi-Shah's Gujarat itself, have opted out of the PMFBY scheme because of its uselessness. The Prime Minister has claimed that cheap credit is being given to small farmers, but this method which is in place from even before he took over, excludes millions of

tenant cultivators. No relief or loan waiver has been given even in times of the Covid Pandemic when farmers have suffered huge income losses.

Yet again the lie that the Minimum Support Price (MSP) has been increased to 1.5 times the cost of production was peddled from the Red Fort while the Government has not implemented the C2+50% formula as recommended by the National Commission on Farmers. It is also to be noted that procurement at even this MSP which is in most crops 40-50% below C2+50% is not assured. According to a report in October and November 2020, in 11 major agricultural states farmers got about Rs 1,900 crore less than MSP for crops sold in those two months…

The costs of all agricultural inputs, especially the back-breaking increases in diesel, petrol and fertilisers are making agriculture unviable. The PM-Kisan scheme is pittance when compared to the increase in production costs and loss of incomes for which the BJP Government's policies are solely responsible. In reality the small farmers and tenant cultivators are the worst-hit by the BJP Government's policies.

PRIME MINISTER'S LIES ON PMFBY EXPOSED

PM Modi chose to draw the nation's attention to the Pradhan Mantri Fasal Bima Yojana (PMFBY) during his speech. He claimed that the country's small farmers are the resolve and mantra for the government and are the nation's pride. In that context, he sought to showcase PMFBY as an effort to increase the power of the small farmer.

The reality of PMFBY is diametrically opposite. This reality exposes the hype being made about this crop insurance scheme right from the beginning of its launch. The story is as false and cruel as the MSP story, where again, the PM made false claims standing right under our national flag.

In PMFBY, the latest figures show that private insurance companies collected in 2018-19 and 2019-20 Rs 31,905.51 crore as gross premium from farmers, state governments and the central government, while the claims paid out amounted to Rs 21,937.95 crore, with a margin of 10,000 crore rupees left for the private insurance corporations to operate and profiteer, over just two years. The insurance claims of lakhs of farmers were never settled.

The number of farmers covered under this scheme has decreased significantly year after year. For instance, during the Kharif season, the number of farmers covered stood at 21.66 lakh in 2018, 20.05 lakh in 2019, 16.79 lakh in 2020 and only 12.31 lakh in 2021 (down by 57 per cent over four years). The story of decline in coverage exists in the Rabi season, too, year after year.

The number of agricultural crops covered by insurance in 2018 Kharif was 38, which decreased to 28 crops by 2021 Kharif. In the case of horticultural crops, it fell from 57 crops in 2018 to 45 in 2021. The area insured during Kharif 2018 was 2.78 crore hectares, which saw a significant decline to 1.71 crore hectares in Kharif 2021. These numbers reveal the real story regarding the failed PMFBY. It was shocking to see the prime minister mention this scheme as one that had increased the power of the small farmer.

AIF CLAIMS OF MODI GOVERNMENT EXPOSED

SKM also exposed the complete picture of the Agriculture Infrastructure Fund (AIF) under the so-called Atmanirbhar Bharat Package. There is simply nothing like a one lakh crore fund allocated by the central government for the same, contrary to its flashing of big numbers. Weakening the mandi system through anti-farmer laws and then saying that the government will facilitate borrowing by the mandis under AIF is just yet another *jumla* announced by the union cabinet. The Union Agriculture Minister saying that the laws will not be repealed, but mandis will be strengthened through AIF, is indeed ironic.

For three years in a row, in his Independence Day speeches, the Prime Minister had talked about 'infrastructure' investments to the tune of 100 lakh crore rupees. In 2019, it was about 'Modern Infrastructure' and a decision to invest 100 lakh crore rupees in the same. In 2020, it was about 'National Infrastructure Pipeline Project', and Modi announced that 110 lakh crore would be spent on this project. In this speech, there was also a reference to the Agriculture Infrastructure Fund (AIF) announced during the first Covid pandemic lockdown, and he had claimed that the Indian Government had 'sanctioned' one lakh crore rupees for this. 'This infrastructure will be for the welfare of the farmers and they will be able to get better prices for their produce, and will be able to sell their produce in foreign markets', Modi had claimed. Now, this year, it is the 'Gati Shakti' National Infrastructure Master Plan as a 'scheme of more than 100 lakh crore rupees.'

The statements of the Prime Minister stand exposed when we look at the reality of the Agriculture Infrastructure Fund, a year after its pompous announcement. AIF is a 13-year scheme, incidentally with disbursements till 2023-24. As of 6 August 2021, only Rs 4503 crore has been sanctioned under AIF for 6524 projects, including 'in-principle' sanctions (4.5 per cent of the so-called 'sanction' announced last year). As per a Rajya Sabha response on 23 July 2021, only 746 crore rupees have actually been disbursed (0.75 per cent of the grand announcement)!

When the Modi government stands by its pro-corporate agriculture laws that undermine the whole legal framework of the APMC market yards to make them collapse, merely allowing APMCs to access some more loans is a meaningless gesture. In the six months during which the three Farm Laws were in operation before the Supreme Court suspended them, the trade-in of most APMC market yards collapsed by almost half and their revenues dropped drastically. The Centre has shown that it has no commitment to build and expand the public market and storage infrastructure for small farmers' benefit and is bent on facilitating the Adanis, Walmart and Reliance to build private markets, storage and processing facilities.

It is well-known that the Gautam Adani conglomerate is the dominant multinational corporation in this sphere. Adani already has control over one-third of India's port volumes. It has recently tied up with Flipkart/Walmart to create the country's largest warehousing facility for the e-commerce giant. Adani Agri Logistics Limited (AALL) has signed an exclusive service agreement with the Food Corporation of India. It is worth noting that Adani's Base Depots are declared as notified 'market yards'. AAAL is the largest player with a 45 per cent market share in modern Agri storage infrastructure. Meanwhile, Adani Wilmar is into food processing. The corporation's ambitions to dominate the food supply chains are notorious.

19 OPPOSITION PARTIES BACK FARMERS' STRUGGLE

On 20 August, 19 opposition parties jointly put out a statement announcing nationwide protests from 20 to 30 September on 11 burning demands of the country. One of the demands was to 'repeal the three anti-agriculture laws and compulsorily guarantee MSP to farmers'. The statement said, 'The historic struggle by our farmers continues into the ninth month now, with the government being obdurate in not repealing the three anti-farmer Laws and compulsorily guaranteeing and giving MSP to the farmers. We, the undersigned, reiterate our support to the struggle launched by the farmers under the banner of the Samyukta Kisan Morcha.'

The Opposition parties' statement further says, 'The destruction of the Indian economy, with deepening recession, is pushing crores of our people into joblessness, escalating the levels of poverty and hunger. The run-away inflation and price rise is adding to people's woes and destroying livelihoods ....The destruction of the economy is accompanied by a mega loot of our national assets; large-scale privatization of the public sector, including banks and financial services; the privatization of our mineral resources and public utilities to benefit the cronies of the Prime Minister. This will be strongly resisted.'

The statement also demands, 'Stop and reverse the unbridled privatization of the public sector; repeal the Labour Codes which dilute the rights of labour and the working class. Restore the rights of the working people to protest and for wage bargaining ....Withdraw unprecedented hikes in central excise duties on petroleum and diesel, reduce prices of cooking gas and essential commodities, particularly cooking oil and control galloping inflation ....Vastly enlarge MGNREGA with increasing guarantee for 200 days with at least doubling of wages. Legislate an urban employment guarantee programme on similar lines.'

After giving the nationwide call for protests from 20 to 30 September, the statement ends by saying, 'We, the leaders of nineteen opposition parties, call upon the people of India to rise to the occasion to defend our secular, democratic republican order with all our might. Save India today, so that we can change it for the better tomorrow.'

INTERNATIONAL SUPPORT WIDENS

On our Independence Day, US farmers extended a message of solidarity with protesting Indian farmers. The US counterparts of the protestors here described their suffering and distress in a free market policy environment that has impoverished farmers there while making corporations richer and capitalists wealthier. Their story of near-extinction is a good lesson for Indian farmers to learn from.

To extend their support and solidarity to the protesting farmers on this Independence Day, sleep-out events were organized in different parts of the world by the Indian diaspora. This included Vancouver, London, San Jose, Seattle, Toronto, Vienna, etc. At the well-known Westminster Bridge over the River Thames in London, a huge banner was unfurled that demanded Prime Minister Narendra Modi's resignation.

20. SKM NATIONAL CONVENTION GIVES CALL FOR BHARAT BANDH

26 August 2021 marked the completion of nine months of the farmers' movement. On this day, the first-ever National Convention of the SKM began at Singhu border near Delhi, and it concluded the next day, on 27 August. Over 2000 delegates from hundreds of organizations from 22 states attended. They included not only delegates from hundreds of kisan organizations, but also leaders of various trade unions, and organizations of agricultural workers, women, students, youth, dalits, adivasis and other marginalized sections. It was a microcosm of India that attended this meet. This convention hammered yet another nail into the package of lies that the Modi regime was feeding the nation.

INAUGURAL SESSION

The convention began by paying homage to the 600 martyrs of this farmers' struggle thus far. It was inaugurated by Rakesh Tikait, who reaffirmed the resolve of farmers to continue the peaceful protest till all the demands were met. Ashish Mittal, Convenor of the Organising Committee, placed the main draft resolution calling for intensification and expansion of the struggle until the three Farm Laws are repealed, the Electricity Amendment Bill is withdrawn, and a legal guarantee to an MSP @C2+50% is given.

The inaugural session on the above farmers' issues was addressed by prominent leaders like Atul Kumar Anjaan, Darshan Pal, Gurnam Singh Charuni, Hannan Mollah, Jagjit Singh Dallewal, Joginder Singh Ugrahan, Medha Patkar, Rajaram Singh, Shivkumar Sharma, Vadde Sobhanadreeswara Rao, Yogendra Yadav, and others.

AIKS general secretary Hannan Mollah underlined the truly historic nature of this united SKM-led farmers' struggle, the like of which has never been seen since Independence. It is directed against the alliance of the BJP-RSS central government and the corporate lobby, which was bent on selling off the country, and attacking democracy, secularism, and the Constitution itself. The peasantry in this struggle hailed from all religions, castes and regions. Over the last nine months, the struggle had strongly countered both repression and defamation from the RSS-BJP. The farmers were fighting not only for themselves, but also for the people of the entire country, since the Farm Laws would destroy everyone. The working class and other sections had been supporting the SKM-led struggle, and the SKM in turn was also supporting their struggles, because the Modi regime was leading an all-round attack on all sections of the working people. In the end, he called for a massive campaign to ensure the political defeat of the BJP, in which the Muzaffarnagar rally on 5 September and the Bharat Bandh on 27 September would play a crucial role.

BROAD SUPPORT

This session on farmers' issues was followed by separate sessions addressed by leaders of the working class; agricultural workers, Dalits and Adivasis; women, student and youth organizations. The distinguishing feature of this convention was that it was a manifestation of worker-peasant unity and the unity of all exploited and oppressed sections.

Among those from various organizations who addressed these sessions were AIAWU general secretary B. Venkat, AIDWA general secretary Mariam Dhawale, CITU president K. Hemalata, and SFI joint secretary Dipsita Dhar. As AIKS president I, along with Haryana vice president Inderjit Singh were in the presidium of different sessions. More than 100 delegates of the AIDWA,

AIAWU, AIKS, CITU, DYFI, and SFI participated in this national convention.

Resolutions were unanimously adopted expressing solidarity and support to the struggles on burning issues like the four Labour Codes, alarming unemployment and hunger, expansion of days and wages under MGNREGA, implementation of the Forest Rights Act, against displacement of tribals by corporates, massive price rise of diesel, petrol, gas and other essential commodities, efforts to dismantle the PDS, atrocities on women, and privatization of education and the health system.

Two more important resolutions – one against the divisive communalism of the RSS-BJP combine and the other against privatization and sale of the country to the corporates by the Modi regime – were unanimously adopted by the convention.

The last session of the convention was devoted to the expansion and intensification of the farmers' struggle. Several farmer leaders from all over the country placed their views.

CLARION CALL TO ACTION

The SKM national convention unanimously adopted the main resolution, which gave the following three-point clarion call to action:

1. Make the Bharat Bandh on 27 September a success,
2. Make the Muzaffarnagar Kisan Mazdoor Mahapanchayat of lakhs of farmers and workers on 5 September a massive success. This would inaugurate Mission Uttar Pradesh-Uttarakhand.
3. Form joint committees of the SKM in all states and districts to ensure a pan-India expansion and intensification of the farmers' struggle.

PUNJAB SUGARCANE FARMERS WIN DEMANDS AFTER STRUGGLE

The big victory of the sugarcane farmers of Punjab on 24 August set the tone for the SKM National Convention. In the third round of talks held between farmer union leaders and the Punjab government, the Punjab Chief Minister announced that the government would increase the sugarcane price to Rs 360 per quintal. This significant increase of Rs 50 per quintal was a major achievement of the farmers' struggle. Sugarcane farmers of Punjab fought a collective battle over five days in Jalandhar, blocking rail and road traffic from 20 August. Farmer leaders thanked all the protestors, including the ones running the langars. They also thanked the people who cooperated, despite the inconvenience caused to them. They announced that the protests would end and urged all protesting farmers to return to the Delhi morchas and strengthen them.

In another welcome development, the Tamil Nadu State Legislature passed a resolution against the three anti-farmer, pro-corporate black laws of the Modi government. Several state governments had supported the farmers' struggle in diverse ways.

SKM expressed its sincere condolences at the passing away of the renowned scholar-activist Gail Omvedt. It said that her writings and activism contributed immensely to all the peoples' movements, especially the movements of Dalits, Bahujan, women and landless farmers.

There was a lathi-charge on farmers in Amritsar, where they were protesting against the PM's virtual speech in an inauguration of a modernization of Jallianwala Bagh. Thousands of youth had assembled, wanting to go to the Jallianwala Bagh massacre site. But they were stopped by the police. The youth challenged Narendra Modi's moral right to get involved in this event.

21. MUZAFFARNAGAR TOWN TURNS INTO RALLY GROUND

The ten lakh-strong SKM-led Kisan Mazdoor Mahapanchayat at Muzaffarnagar in Uttar Pradesh on 5 September 2021, forced even the most pro-establishment newspaper like *The Times of India* to pen its lead editorial on the mammoth rally. The *Hindustan Times* and several other national dailies also ran editorials on the rally. On 5 and 6 September, of course, almost all sections of the electronic and print media fell over one another to cover this unprecedented congregation of farmers in their lead headlines and on their front pages. It was indeed a massive Jan Sailab – a massive flood of people.

UNPRECEDENTED MAHAPANCHAYAT

The entire town of Muzaffarnagar had literally turned into a rally ground. Farmers in massive numbers started coming from the previous evening itself. The huge GIC ground, with a capacity of around one lakh, started overflowing with enthusiastic and determined farmers from the early morning. The ground could accommodate only one-tenth of the farmers, and nine-tenths of them overfilled all the main roads of the city. Lakhs of farmers listened to the speeches on the streets, where a public address system had been set up for several kilometres around the ground. Hundreds of langars and medical camps had been set up to help the farmers.

There was an unending flow of people, tractors, buses and cars still coming into Muzaffarnagar till afternoon. An ocean of people cutting across states, religions, castes, regions and languages came together to send a loud and clear message to the BJP-RSS governments at the centre and state-led by Modi, Shah and Yogi, and to their crony corporates like the Ambanis and the Adanis. The Kisan Mazdoor Mahapanchayat got unprecedented support from all sections of society – farmers, workers, agricultural labourers, employees, small traders, women, youth and students. The rally raised the resounding slogans of Kisan-Mazdoor Unity and called for the defeat of the anti-farmer, anti-people and anti-national BJP-RSS government.

Lakhs of farmers had come from Uttar Pradesh, Uttarakhand, Haryana, Punjab, Madhya Pradesh, and Rajasthan. Contingents also came from Andhra Pradesh, Assam, Bihar, Karnataka, Kerala, Maharashtra, Tamil Nadu, Telangana, West Bengal, and other states. Women and youth farmers had come in massive numbers. The farmers were carrying thousands of national flags and flags of their own farmers' organizations. It was a very colourful spectacle of green, red, yellow, white and blue flags – all colours except saffron!

POLITICAL SIGNIFICANCE

This mega rally showed that the battle for the country had moved from Punjab and Haryana straight to the Hindi heartland. It was politically significant for five main reasons.

First, it reiterated the call given by the SKM's National Convention for a Bharat Bandh on 27 September. Overall, the rally was a massive demonstration of people's discontent with the incumbent government. Hectic preparations were launched all over the country to reach out to all progressive, democratic, and secular forces to ensure that the Bharat Bandh against the BJP-RSS regime became a massive success. Every speaker in the rally stressed the vital significance of making the Bharat Bandh successful.

Second, the rally inaugurated Mission Uttar Pradesh-Uttarakhand, which called not only for strengthening the farmers' struggle for the repeal of the three Farm Laws and a central law guaranteeing MSP @ C2+50% but also resolved to leave no stone unturned to ensure the resounding defeat of the BJP in the coming state assembly elections. Some of the details of this Mission were worked out in an SKM meeting in Lucknow soon after on 9-10 September.

Third, this united rally powerfully countered the divisive memories of the ghastly Muzaffarnagar communal riots engineered by the RSS-BJP in 2013. The communal polarization resulting from this all over North India was one of the major factors that swept the BJP to power at the Centre in 2014 and UP in 2017. The most effective symbol of unity manifested at the rally was the scene of Naresh Tikait and Ghulam Mohammad Jaula sitting together on the stage. All speakers at the rally charged that the BJP government of Uttar Pradesh is using the notorious British policy of 'Divide and Rule' based on divisions around religion and caste. The Kisan-Mazdoor unity agenda would triumph over the communal and casteist politics of the RSS-BJP, and the farmers would never allow communal riots to happen again.

Tens of thousands of Muslims from UP not only took part in the rally, but many Muslims also organized a lot of langars and other forms of Seva for the farmers going to Muzaffarnagar. Even mosques made arrangements for people's accommodation, where Hindu and Sikh farmers stayed at night. This further cemented ties between the two communities. Many farmers in the region were talking about the hospitality extended by Muslims. They were clearly touched.

Fourth, almost all major speakers directly accused the Modi government of selling off the entire country to the domestic and foreign corporate lobby through its shameless National Monetization Pipeline and other disastrous measures toward privatization of innumerable public sector concerns. They also supported the working class demand for repeal of the four Labour Codes. They denounced the Modi regime for the massive price hike of diesel, petrol, cooking gas and other essential commodities, burgeoning unemployment and the collapse of the PDS.

Thus, the SKM's Mahapanchayat raised issues of sectors beyond agriculture, just as its National Convention had done ten days ago on 26-27 August. The farmers' struggle was proving to be much more than just the demand to revoke the three Farm Laws and for an MSP guarantee. It had become the most significant movement not just to save but also to deepen our democracy and secularism and to defend our Constitution.

Fifth, the speakers charged that the promises made by the Yogi government to the farmers had not been fulfilled. Even 20 per cent of the promised procurement had not been done. The Uttar Pradesh government had promised a loan waiver for 86 lakh farmers, while only 45 lakh farmers had received only a very partial loan waiver. In Uttar Pradesh, crop insurance compensation was paid to 72 lakh farmers in 2016-17, while in 2019-20, only 47 lakh farmers were paid the same, but crop insurance companies earned a whopping profit of Rs 2,508 crore. The Union Government agency CACP had found that in 2017, the cost of sugarcane was Rs 383 per quintal, but farmers were paid only Rs 325 per quintal, and sugar mills owed farmers over Rs 13,000 crore. The rally announced an agitation demanding a rate of Rs 450 per quintal for sugarcane that was promised by the Yogi government.

MAGNIFICENT MANIFESTATION OF UNITY

Some of the slogans given in this rally indicated its fiery fighting spirit. *Daam nahin to vote nahin* (no fair price, no vote) – *Vote pe chot* (hit the vote) – *Woh todenge, hum jodenge* (they will try to break us, we will stand united). The double slogan from Mahendra Singh Tikait's time came into play: *Har Har Mahadev* and *Allah Hu Akbar*. At the same time, *Jo Bole So Nihal, Sat Sri Akal* and *Wahe Guru Ji Da Khalsa, Wahe Guru Ji Di Fateh* resounded on the stage.

The speakers from Karnataka, Kerala, and Tamil Nadu, who spoke in their mother tongues, were wildly cheered by the crowd, although they could not understand a word of what they said. Several references by speakers to Shaheed-e-Azam Bhagat Singh, Shaheed Ashfaqullah Khan, Dr Babasaheb Ambedkar, Swami Sahajanand Saraswati, and other icons drew loud applause. It was a magnificent manifestation of the unity and the determination of the peasantry of India.

All the prominent SKM leaders and leaders from all the states present addressed the public meeting. They also included several women and youth speakers. Prominent among them were Amrita Kundu, Ashish Mittal, Balbir Singh Rajewal, Baldev Singh Nihalgarh, Darshan Pal, Dharmendra Malik, D.P. Singh, Gurnam Singh Charuni, Hannan Mollah, Harmeet Singh Kadian, Jagjit Singh Dallewal, Jasbir Kaur, Jagmati Sangwan, Joginder Singh Ugrahan, Koth, Kulwant Singh Sandhu, Manjit Singh Dhaner, Manjit Rai, Medha Patkar, Naresh Tikait, Rajesh Singh Chauhan, Rajveer Singh Jadaun, Rakesh Tikait, Ranjeet Raju, Ruldu Singh Mansa, Satnam Singh Ajnala, Satyavan, Shivkumar Sharma 'Kakkaji', Sonia Maan, Sunilam, Suresh, Tajinder Singh Virk, Yogendra Yadav, Yudhvir Singh, and several other leaders.

The AIKS mobilization in this rally was very impressive. Red flags of the AIKS could be seen everywhere. Thousands of farmers were mobilized by the AIKS from its state units in Haryana, Madhya Pradesh, Punjab, Rajasthan, Uttarakhand, Uttar Pradesh, along with a spirited contingent from far-off Assam. A large contingent of the AIKS from Bihar came at the same time to Delhi and stayed for a week at the Ghazipur border. Thousands of activists of the AIKS, CITU, AIAWU, AIDWA, DYFI and SFI from all the above states worked hard for this success.

The AIKS made concerted preparations to mobilize thousands of farmers for this rally. AIKS leaders Amra Ram, Badal Saroj, Bharat Singh, Chandrapal Singh, D.P. Singh, Gangadhar Nautiyal, Hannan Mollah, Inderjit Singh, Major Singh Punnewal, Mukut Singh, N.K. Shukla, P. Krishnaprasad, Sumit, Vijoo Krishnan, myself, and others attended several meetings in the above states to mobilize the AIKS in large numbers for this Kisan Mazdoor Mahapanchayat.

The SKM congratulated and thanked the lakhs of farmers who braved all the obstructions placed by the BJP's Yogi government and called upon them to take the torch of the farmers' movement to every nook and corner of India until victory is achieved.

22. THE VICTORIOUS KARNAL STRUGGLE

Haryana's BJP-JJP government was anti-farmer right from the beginning of the farmers' movement. The Haryana government placed numerous obstacles in the path of convoys of protesting farmers headed to the national capital in November 2020 to present their demands to the union government. The state government made numerous illegal detentions and arrests in Haryana, along with violence through tear gas shells and water cannons unleashed on farmers headed to Delhi.

Subsequently, the state government filed cases on around 48,000 farmers as though it was waging war against its own people. The administration filed over 150 different cases and two cases of sedition against protesting farmers. In these cases, the government named 687 protesters by name and filed cases against 47,000 unknown persons as accused. The Haryana government attacked farmers protesting against the Annapurna Utsav promotion gimmicks by slapping more cases on them. And these cases were being slapped for burning empty grain bags on which anti-farmer faces of BJP and JJP leaders Modi, Khattar and Chautala were printed. The nervousness of the Khattar government was apparent even as the farmers' movement gained greater momentum. It was clear that BJP and JJP leaders in the state were fearful of facing the public and being held accountable for their anti-farmer actions.

Uttar Pradesh's BJP government was no less in its anti-people stance. As the farmers' movement got stronger in the state, the Yogi Adityanath government got more nervous. Cases were filed against several protesting farmers in UP. In just one district, Pilibhit, FIRs were registered against 58 farmers who participated in a peaceful black flag protest against a state Minister. Farmer unions in the state demanded the withdrawal of these cases.

Innumerable peaceful black flag demonstrations by farmers

against BJP's union and state Ministers, MPs, MLAs and others continued unabated in Haryana, Punjab, Uttar Pradesh, Uttarakhand, Rajasthan, Madhya Pradesh and Delhi. They were too numerous to recount.

SKM also condemned the latest move by the Haryana government to amend the Land Acquisition Act (LARR 2013) in a way that opens the floodgates of compulsory acquisition under the garb of PPP without farmers' consent. This amendment sought to bring, from the backdoor, the anti-farmer amendments that the Modi government had failed to carry out in 2015. It undermined the significant LARR law that Parliament unanimously passed in 2013.

'BREAK THEIR HEADS'

On 28 August, the very next day after the successful conclusion of the SKM's National Convention, brutal repression was unleashed by the BJP-JJP government, its administration and its police in Haryana on peaceful farmer protestors at the Bastara toll plaza in Karnal. They had gathered to peacefully give slogans and show black flags to BJP chief minister Manohar Lal Khattar, who had come to attend a programme in Karnal. Scores of farmers were seriously injured and were bleeding profusely in the violence unleashed by the police.

The worst aspect was the disgraceful orders of the SDM Ayush Sinha to the police force deployed in Karnal to 'break the heads' of the protestors. The video of him giving these orders went viral. It was evident that the SDM could not have given such draconian orders without political instigation from the top. The next day, police cases were lodged against 100 farmers.

On the same night of 28 August, Sushil Kajal, a 55 year-old farmer of Village Raipur Jatan, District Karnal, who received severe blows in the police lathi-charge, died. He was cremated at

11 am on the morning of 29 August, without any post mortem being conducted. He was a regular participant in this farmers' struggle right from the beginning.

Sushil Kajal became a martyr of the bloodthirsty BJP-JJP state government of Haryana.

VALIANT RESISTANCE BY FARMERS

The SKM gave a call to block roads everywhere to condemn this repression and the death of Sushil Kajal. Farmers from all over Haryana, Punjab, Uttar Pradesh, Uttarakhand, Rajasthan, Madhya Pradesh and other states responded to this call. In several places, the effigies of the Haryana chief minister were burnt.

Khattar brushed aside the barbaric and illegal instructions of Ayush Sinha as only a wrong choice of words! This clearly pointed the needle of suspicion of the political direction of this brutal attack to the CM himself. On the other hand, BJP leader and Meghalaya Governor Satya Pal Malik hinted that if the Khattar government did not dismiss the official immediately, it could only be assumed that the official was acting on instructions from elsewhere.

A massive SKM Kisan Panchayat organized in the Gharonda grain market in Karnal issued an ultimatum to the Haryana government and gave the deadline of 6 September. The farmers wanted the BJP-JJP government to take strong action against SDM Ayush Sinha by filing a case of murder charges on him and dismissing him immediately. SKM also demanded the immediate and unconditional withdrawal of all police cases by the Haryana government.

The AIKS, in two press releases issued on consecutive days, denounced the repression by the Haryana government and its police, mourned the death of martyr Sushil Kajal, and demanded the immediate dismissal of the SDM Ayush Sinha; the institution of a case under IPC 302 against Ayush Sinha; a judicial enquiry into the police atrocities, with specific terms of reference to also expose the political masters behind such disgraceful orders, which were a reminder of the orders of the hated British General Dyer and the Jallianwala Bagh massacre; and the Supreme Court to take suo moto cognisance of the above shocking video of SDM Ayush Sinha and immediately punish all those guilty, including the political leaders who were responsible for this brutal repression.

The AIKS warned the BJP-JJP state government that the current unprecedented farmers' struggle could never be suppressed by such inhuman acts of the anti-people government. These efforts at repression would only strengthen the farmers' resolve and determination. The AIKS called upon all its units across the country to condemn this barbaric repression in Haryana and the killing of Sushil Kajal by organizing immediate nationwide protest demonstrations.

On 7 September, another massive one lakh strong SKM rally of farmers was held at Karnal in Haryana. In a shameful and cowardly act, the district administration imposed Section 144, shut down the internet in Karnal and surrounding districts, and threatened to charge the protestors with Section 188 IPC. A troop of 40 companies of security forces, including ten companies of the Central Armed Police Force (CAPF), were stationed in Karnal.

Despite all this, one lakh farmers gathered. They denounced the BJP-JJP state government in Haryana and demanded the dismissal of and filing of murder charges against SDM Ayush Sinha, who had given instructions to the police to 'break people's heads'. But far from dismissing him, he was transferred and promoted with the blessings of BJP-JJP bigwigs!

GOVERNMENT FORCED TO BEND

The four-day-long SKM gherao by thousands of farmers of the Karnal Mini Secretariat began on 7 September. Treating all repressive measures with the contempt that they deserved, the huge mass of farmers marched to the Mini Secretariat. The police did not dare to stop such a huge mass. Thousands of farmers, including women, camped outside for four days and nights. The gherao was addressed by SKM leaders and by several leaders of the Haryana farm unions. Three rounds of talks with the administration failed. The farmers remained unbending. At last, on 11 September, it was the state government that was forced to bend. It was a major victory for the united farmers' struggle.

The Khattar government agreed to suspend SDM Ayush Sinha, IAS, the official who ordered the 'breaking of farmers' heads' on 28 August. A judicial inquiry would be held under a retired High Court Judge who would look into Ayush Sinha's role and the police violence that resulted in martyr Sushil Kajal's death, and grievous injury to several others. The probe would be completed within a month. The government also agreed to a sizable compensation to the family of Sushil Kajal and support in the form of two jobs on sanctioned vacant posts to his family members. Compensation would also be given to the farmers injured in the violence. All police cases against farmers would be withdrawn. With this agreement between the farmers and the administration, the Karnal gherao ended in the same victorious fashion as the previous dharnas in Hisar, Tohana and Sirsa in Haryana.

SKM AND AIKS LEADERS COME OUT IN FULL SUPPORT

All SKM leaders, including Atul Kumar Anjaan, Balbir Singh Rajewal, Darshan Pal, Gurnam Singh Charuni, Jagjit Singh Dallewal, Joginder Singh Ugrahan, Rakesh Tikait, Yogendra Yadav, myself, and others provided solid backing to the Karnal gherao with our active participation. On behalf of the AIKS – Inderjit Singh, P. Krishnaprasad, Kuldeep Singh, Mahipal, Phool Singh Sheokand, Sumit, Master Sher Singh, and others were an integral part of this struggle. AIAWU general secretary B. Venkat and joint secretary V. Sivadasan, MP, also came to Karnal in support. Inderjit Singh and Phool Singh Sheokand represented the AIKS in the 14 member team that negotiated with the administration.

An AIKS delegation visited the family members of martyr Sushil Kajal in his village on 31 August. It provided immediate relief of Rs 1 lakh to the victim's family from its Kisan Struggle Fund. The delegation comprised AIKS finance secretary P. Krishnaprasad, state president Phool Singh Sheokand, state secretary Sumit, district president Surender Malik, Ashok Arora, CITU district secretary Jagpal Rana, and AIDWA district secretary Jasoda.

The team's findings were reported in an AIKS press conference that Hannan Mollah and P. Krishnaprasad addressed. Immediately after the 28 August attacks, the AIKS released two strong press releases denouncing the repression.

The delegation met Sushil's mother Murti Devi and wife Sudesh Devi. The mother said Sushil had injuries at the back of his head and shoulder and was in severe pain. He was not admitted to the hospital by the police, hence was forced to come home. He died in the night and there was swelling on his face and abdomen with skin turned bluish in colour. The wife said Sushil was part of the farmers' struggle during the last nine months and after his death no police or revenue officers visited the family. Farmer leaders at Bastara toll plaza also said that a group of policemen severely beat Sushil. Police did not allow them to take him to the hospital, and those who were severely injured were also forced to leave the hospital after first aid.

The AIKS delegation came to the conclusion that Sushil Kajal was murdered due to the severe lathi-charge by the Haryana police, resulting in internal injuries and bleeding. Instead of taking him to hospital and ensuring treatment to save his life, the police did the criminal act of not allowing him to get admitted to hospital. The body was cremated in the village without a post mortem on 29 August. The Superintendent of Police Ganga Ram Puniya claimed that the death was due to a heart attack. How could the police state the cause of death without a post mortem? This was a deliberate attempt to hide the truth and protect the culprits.

CPI(M) GENERAL SECRETARY MEETS FAMILY OF MARTYR

On 12 September, a CPI(M) delegation led by general secretary Sitaram Yechury visited Raipur Jatan village and met the family of Sushil Kajal. He was accompanied by Polit Bureau member Nilotpal Basu and central committee member Jogendra Sharma. Others present were AIKS state vice president Inderjit Singh, AIDWA vice president Jagmati Sangwan, Karnal party district secretary Ashok Arora, Panipat district secretary Sunil Dutt, CITU leader Jagpal, and others.

Sitaram Yechury saluted the bravery of the mother, who said that she would not cry over the loss of her son. Sharing their grief, he also appreciated the courage exhibited by Sudesh, wife of martyr Sushil, who joined the Kisan morcha on 7 September. He assured the aggrieved family that his Party would try its best on all forums to see that the agreement between the government and SKM on 11 September was executed in both letter and spirit.

Later, addressing a media conference, Sitaram said that the Haryana government had to accept the demands due to the massive farmers' mobilization. He said the Modi-led BJP regime was on the defensive in the face of rising discontent among the people, as was seen in the assembly elections in some states held a few months ago. The removal of four chief ministers of BJP-ruled states in a row, including Gujarat, is testimony enough to the dwindling popularity of this party. He reiterated the support extended to the Bharat Bandh on 27 September by the opposition parties.

23. HISTORIC BHARAT BANDH RATTLES BJP-RSS REGIME

The Bharat Bandh on 27 September 2021 was truly historic. In breadth, sweep and intensity, it surpassed the earlier two Bharat Bandhs in solidarity with the unprecedented farmers' struggle, on 8 December 2020 and 26 March 2021. The SKM called it to coincide with the completion of 10 months and 305 days of this struggle, which led to 605 Kisan martyrs thus far.

It was exactly a year ago, on 27 September 2020, that President Ram Nath Kovind had given presidential assent to the three Farm Laws, which were rammed through Parliament by the Modi regime by murdering parliamentary democracy, on 17 September in the Lok Sabha (as a birthday present to himself and his crony corporates) and on 20 September in the Rajya Sabha. On 29 September, the same government rammed through Parliament three of the four Labour Codes. The Modi regime had enacted the first Code on Wages in 2019.

Impressive state level joint conventions and press conferences were held to plan the Bharat Bandh. All constituents of the SKM and thousands of activists of other organizations participated in these. Central and state leaders of the AIKS, CITU, AIAWU, AIDWA, DYFI, and SFI were in the forefront of organizing these joint conventions.

Thousands of district, tehsil, city, town and village level meetings were held to propagate the Bandh call. Lakhs and lakhs of leaflets were distributed to the people. This spread the message of the Bandh to millions of people across the country. The SKM announced that the Bandh will be from 6 am to 4 pm, with only essential services excluded.

The SKM also extended active support to the All India Strike of Scheme Workers on 24 September, which had massive participation of Anganwadi, ASHA, MDM, NCLP, SSA and NHM workers. These workers were demanding regularization of their services as workers, with provision of minimum wages, in addition to stopping privatization of public sector units and services and withdrawal of the four Labour Codes. SKM recognized that these scheme workers delivering basic services of nutrition, healthcare, early childhood care and education in even remote parts of the country, were mainly women, were being exploited and did not get even sustenance level allowances. These workers were at the frontline of fighting the Covid pandemic at risk to their own lives. The SKM greeted lakhs of these workers and expressed full solidarity with their strike.

POLITICAL SUPPORT

The Bharat Bandh was actively supported by several opposition parties, central trade unions, and several organisations of agricultural workers, employees, traders, transporters, women, youth, students, teachers, and lawyers. Thousands of images of the Bharat Bandh success came on the SKM, AIKS, CITU and other social media. All sections of the mainstream print and electronic media were forced to give coverage to this massive action.

The state governments that publicly supported the Bharat Bandh were the LDF government of Kerala, the DMK government of Tamil Nadu, the YSR Congress government of Andhra Pradesh, the JMM-led government of Jharkhand and the Congress government of Punjab. Left Parties like the CPI(M), CPI, AIFB, RSP, CPI-ML (Liberation), CPI-ML (ND), SUCI (C), in addition to many other parties like INC, AAP, SP, TDP, NCP, DMK, YSRCP, JMM, RJD, JD(S), BSP, SAD-Samyukt, Swaraj India and others extended their support to the Bharat Bandh. The Central Trade Unions organized protest rallies at Jantar Mantar in New Delhi and many other centres.

The hypocrisy of the TMC regime in West Bengal was on full display when, on the one hand, it made empty noises in support of the farmers, but on the other, not only opposed the Bandh call but also made its police rain blows on CPI(M) and Left activists on the Bandh day. The BJP government in Tripura too launched severe repressive attacks on the CPI(M) and the Left.

The Bharat Bandh was clearly directed against the anti-people and pro-corporate policies and also the communal and authoritarian conspiracies of the BJP-RSS regime led by Modi and Shah. Some of the main issues that were highlighted in the Bharat Bandh were: Repeal of the three Farm Laws and the four Labour Codes; withdrawal of the Electricity Amendment Bill; a central law to guarantee Minimum Support Price (MSP) for all agricultural produce at one and a half times the comprehensive cost of production (C2+50%); an end to the privatization drive aimed at selling off the public sector and the country to corporates for a pittance; halving the astronomical prices of diesel, petrol, gas and other essential commodities; doubling the days of work and wages in MGNREGA, and extending this scheme to urban areas; and defending democracy, secularism, federalism, and the Constitution against the attacks of the RSS-BJP.

WIDESPREAD RESPONSE

The detailed SKM press statement released on 27 September stated,

> Reports have come in from hundreds of locations from Andhra Pradesh, Assam, Bihar, Chattisgarh, Delhi, Gujarat, Haryana, Himachal Pradesh, Jammu & Kashmir, Jharkhand, Kerala, Karnataka, Madhya Pradesh, Maharashtra, Odisha, Pondicherry, Punjab, Rajasthan, Tamil Nadu, Telangana, Tripura, Uttar Pradesh, Uttarakhand, and West Bengal

about the Bandh, and numerous events to accompany the same. In Punjab alone, there were more than 500 locations in which people gathered to express their support to the Bandh. Similarly, the Bandh witnessed numerous non-farmer associations stand in solidarity with farmers, and also raise their own issues. Lakhs of citizens took part in the Bandh events today.

Life came to a near standstill in several states like Kerala, Punjab, Haryana, Jharkhand and Bihar. Reports indicate that in several parts of southern Assam, Karnataka, Tamil Nadu, Maharashtra, Rajasthan and Uttarakhand, the same was the situation. Scores of protests marked the day in states like Tamilnadu, Telangana, Karnataka, Rajasthan, Uttar Pradesh and Uttarakhand. In Jaipur and Bangalore, capital cities of Rajasthan and Karnataka, tens of thousands of protestors joined protest rallies taken out in the cities. The overall mood across the country was of anger and frustration with BJP-RSS policies that the Modi Government is enforcing, curbing basic freedoms and democracy, and putting most citizens on the path of a survival struggle. It is patently clear that the people of India are tired of the Modi government's adamant, unreasonable and egoistic stand on the protesting farmers' legitimate demands, and anti-people policies in numerous sectors.

The response to this Bandh call was more widespread than before. Nearly all Opposition political parties had extended unconditional support to the Bandh and were in fact keen on not being left out. Trade unions were firmly with the farmers, showcasing the unity of farmers and workers once again. Various trader, merchant and transporter associations, student and youth organizations, women's organizations, taxi and auto unions, teachers' and lawyers' unions, journalists' unions, writers and artists and other progressive groups were firmly with the farmers of the country in this Bandh. People were highly sympathetic to the cause of the 'annadaatas' of India. Even while hundreds of volunteers were detained across the country, the Bandh remained peaceful. The most remarkable aspect of the Bandh was its scale and expanse. Reports of the Bandh emerged from every state of India, and it reached farmers in far and distant places of India.

INTERNATIONAL SOLIDARITY

The farmers' movement and the Bandh call got support from the Indian diaspora in various countries, along with farmers' organizations of other countries.

During Prime Minister Narendra Modi's overseas trip to the USA, supporters of farmers organized protests in Washington DC, right outside the White House. They held up placards that said, 'We Support Farmers', 'No Farmers, No Food, No Future', 'Jai Jawan, Jai Kisan', 'Indian Government, Stop Suppressing Farmers', and so on. Farmers' supporters turned up with flags even in so-called celebration events organized to mark the American trip of PM Modi. Protests were also held near the United Nations building in New York. A Kisan Car Rally was organized in Sacramento, California, to extend support to the protesting farmers. Protests were led by the Indian Workers Association of Great Britain in the United Kingdom, at London, Birmingham and Glasgow, in addition to a protest in Dublin, Ireland. There was a solidarity demonstration by the Indo-Canadian Workers Association at Surrey, and a solidarity walk in Toronto, both places in Canada.

Multiple hashtags pertaining to the farmers' movement trended for a long time in India, where Twitterati also reached out to the United Nations General Assembly's 76th Session President on the farmers' agitation. In the past too, farmer leaders had reached out to the United Nations highlighting the fact that India is violating multiple articles under the UN Declaration on the Rights of Peasants and Other People Working in Rural Areas, adopted by the UN in 2018.

On 28 September, the day after the Bharat Bandh, as per the SKM call, farmers from across the nation observed Shaheed Bhagat Singh Jayanti. Remembrance programmes were held at all SKM morchas and protest sites where youth and students came together in large numbers, and remembered the great son of India who laid down his life in a supreme sacrifice for the values of freedom, democracy, secularism and socialism. Shaheed Bhagat Singh's sacrifice would always inspire the farmers and the people of India in their fight against injustice.

AIKS CONDEMNS GRUESOME ASSAM KILLINGS

The countrywide role and initiative of the AIKS, CITU, AIAWU, AIDWA, DYFI and SFI in the campaign for, and execution of, the Bharat Bandh was impressive. The AIKS statement released on 27 September, expressed its profound happiness and extended hearty congratulations to all sections of the people who made the Bharat Bandh called by the SKM a grand success. Stating that the main slogan of the Bandh was 'Corporate Forces, Hands Off Agriculture, and Modi-Shah Quit Power', the statement concluded by saying, 'The political direction of today's Bharat Bandh is that the last few years of joint struggles with the solid class character of worker-peasant unity now paves the way towards building a larger people's united front against corporate exploitation especially in agriculture, industry and services. Those political parties who stand for protecting corporate interests will face the people's ire and will be pushed back in the face of the emergence of this movement of people's resistance.'

Just before the Bharat Bandh, on 23 September, there came the horrific news of the police of the BJP's Assam government gunning down two Muslim farmers, Saddam Hussain and 12 year-old Sheikh Forid. The AIKS held an immediate press conference in Delhi on 25 September, addressed by general secretary Hannan

Mollah, myself as president, joint secretaries N.K. Shukla and Vijoo Krishnan, and finance secretary P. Krishnaprasad.

The AIKS statement said, 'AIKS expresses shock and anger at the manner in which brute force has been used to forcibly evict thousands of poor peasants in the Dholpur-Gorukhuti area of Sipajhar in Darrang district of Assam. Two farmers are reported to have been killed and many are injured in police firing. The horrific manner of the police action and the brutality inflicted on a farmer already shot dead is a blot on humanity. The eviction drive took place even as a case was pending with the Gauhati High Court on the matter, without even giving enough notice to the people. Constitutional guarantee of equality and security for all citizens is being grossly violated. AIKS demands dismissal of the authorities responsible for the killing, and resignation of the Assam Chief Minister Himanta Biswa Sarma who also holds the Home Affairs portfolio. AIKS demands a judicial enquiry by a sitting Judge of the High Court into the incidents.

'The Chief Minister a couple of days ago, displaying extreme insensitivity, justified the eviction of the farmers who are Bengali Muslims cultivating the land for decades, and expressed happiness as well as complimented the district administration and the Assam police 'for having cleared about 4500 bigha, by evicting 800 households, demolishing four illegal religious structures and a private institution'. How can an elected representative be happy that thousands of people are forcibly evicted without any mutually agreed upon rehabilitation and resettlement plan? The entire eviction drive in the name of 'illegal migrants' is with an ulterior motive of communally polarising the state by pitting communities against one another. If the government was actually promoting a policy of community farming, it could have involved these 800 households who were cultivating the area for decades. After the Haryana BJP government brutally killed a farmer Sushil Kajal, now the Assam BJP government has also followed suit by shooting down two farmers with a sinister agenda.

'It must be noted that the poor peasant households had settled here after displacement due to floods in the Brahmaputra; their lands in the riverine area Kirakara near the Darrang district headquarters Mangaldoi had been washed away. They had been cultivating the land for decades. The humanitarian concern not to brand them as encroachers and allow them to earn their livelihood by ensuring resettlement as well as rehabilitation including provision of cultivable land was clearly lacking in the Assam government's drive. The right of the Muslim peasantry to peacefully earn their livelihood in their own land is being denied.

'AIKS demands a compensation of Rs 25 lakh and job to families of the deceased as well as Rs 5 lakh for the seriously injured. AIKS calls upon all its units to protest against the targeting of Muslim peasants and unleashing of brutal violence on them. We demand an immediate halt to the eviction drive and proper rehabilitation and resettlement of the affected families.'

The SKM also released a similar statement of condemnation. The AIKS and AIAWU twice sent their joint central and state teams to Assam to visit the families of the martyrs. They were led by Vijoo Krishnan, V Sivadasan, MP, Bikash Ranjan Bhattacharya, MP, Suprakash Talukdar, Gajen Barman, Tiken Das and others. On the first visit they gave a sum of one lakh rupees each to the families of the martyrs, and some amount to the injured. On the second visit they distributed blankets worth Rs 5 lakh to all the affected families. This was from the AIKS struggle fund.

NSO SURVEY REVEALS BANKRUPTCY OF MODI REGIME

Two events at this time once again revealed the sheer bankruptcy of the Modi regime vis-a-vis agriculture and farmers. One was the report of the 77th Round Survey of the National Statistical Office (NSO). The second was the MSP declared by the central government for Rabi crops.

For years, the Modi Government had been dangling the elusive goal of 'doubling farmers' income'. The deadline for the promise made in 2016 was to do it in six years, by 2022. That year is already upon us. Instead of legally guaranteeing remunerative MSP on all agricultural produce based on the C2+50% formula, the Modi Government chose to do direct income transfers of a paltry Rs 500 a month as part of the PM Kisan Samman Yojana for land-owning agrarian households. This was done as a pre-election stunt in 2019.

And now, the report card on the Modi government's *jumla* was officially out. NSO's 77th Round Survey showed that over 50 per cent of the agricultural households were in debt, with the farmers' debt increasing by 58 per cent over the last five years. Income from farming had in fact decreased in real terms, with more agricultural income coming in the form of wages or non-farm business than from cultivation. This also confirmed that the remunerative price route was the most direct route to improving farmer incomes.

The 77th Round Survey of NSO on the Situation Assessment of Agricultural Households (data of 2019) clearly showed that the income from farming (crop production and livestock farming) on an average at Rs 5380 per month was not significantly higher than the income for an agricultural household from other sources like wages and non-farm business (at Rs 4838 per month). This was despite the fact that 92.7 per cent of the agricultural households were engaged in crop production during the Kharif season.

Net average receipts from crop production at Rs 3,798 per month were, in fact, lower than wage income at Rs 4,063 per month for agricultural households in India in 2019. Back in 2013, as per the National Sample Survey Office (NSSO) 70th Round Survey, the net receipts from cultivation were Rs 3,081 per month, whereas receipts from wages were Rs 2,071 per month. This clearly showed the decline of farming in the last six years. Moreover, in 15 states, the net receipts from crop production were less than the national average of Rs 3,798 per month, which in itself worked out to a meagre income of around Rs 125 per agricultural household per day. All these were figures for the year 2019. The Covid years 2020 and 2021 hit farmers even harder in numerous ways, depressing their incomes still further.

MSP FOR RABI CROPS AGAIN CHEATS FARMERS

The central government announced the MSP for Rabi crops with the usual rhetoric of 'greatest ever increase in MSP', 'extraordinary favour to farmers', etc. However, the fact was that the government had actually reduced the MSP of Rabi crops in real terms. While the retail inflation stood at 6 per cent, the MSP for wheat and chana (gram) had been increased by 2 per cent and 2.5 per cent only. This meant that in real terms, the MSP of wheat and chana had been reduced by 4 per cent and 3.5 per cent, respectively. The new MSP of Rs 2015 declared for wheat for 2022-23 was equivalent to Rs 1901 when adjusted for inflation, which was Rs 74 less than Rs 1975 declared for wheat for 2021-22. Similarly, the MSP of chana was reduced from Rs 5100 to Rs 4934 in real terms. On the one hand, the farmers were facing the brunt of massively increased prices of diesel, petrol, fertilizers, other agricultural inputs and their daily necessities, and on the other hand, they were becoming poorer as their income was getting reduced.

The government was also deceitfully misusing the term 'Comprehensive Costs', which had always been used to refer to the C2 Cost of Production. As pointed out by farmer bodies since 2018, the government was blatantly deceiving the farmers by using a lower cost measure (A2+FL) and claiming that it was providing MSP at 50 per cent above the comprehensive cost. For example, in 2021-22, the comprehensive cost of production (C2) for wheat was Rs 1467, which was 50 per cent higher than the lower cost (A2+FL) of Rs 960 used by the government.

Finally, without a legal guarantee for MSP, the MSP declared by the government would remain on paper for most of the farmers. Lakhs of farmers, particularly in states where there was no government procurement, had to sell their crops below MSP. Hence, the legal guarantee for MSP had been the longstanding demand of the farmers and one of the key demands of the SKM.

The AIKS, in its statement, condemned the callous manner in which the Narendra Modi-led BJP government announced the MSP for the Rabi Marketing Season 2022-23 without following the C2+50% formula or even taking into account increased costs of inputs and inflation. The statement said,

> The increase in wheat prices is merely 2.03 per cent from Rs 1975 to Rs 2015 per quintal, the lowest increase in 12 years. The MSPs of other crops have a meagre nominal increase ranging from 2.14 per cent to 8.60 per cent, while in real terms in all crops the farmers will suffer huge losses. Besides, only a small section of farmers get to sell their produce at MSP since there is no guaranteed procurement. In the absence of guaranteed procurement, even this MSP is not ensured for farmers. This is precisely the reason why farmers are demanding MSP at C2+50% as a legal right.

CYNICAL CORPORATE LOOT

Apple farmers in Himachal Pradesh led big protests against the government's refusal to ensure remunerative prices for apples and its encouragement to open loot by corporates. This year Adani Agri Fresh fixed the rate of A-grade premium apples at Rs 72 per kg, as against Rs 88 per kg last year. Consequently, most of the farmers ran into big losses. The apple farmers were joined by the farmers growing tomatoes, potatoes, garlic, cauliflower and other crops.

Union Agriculture Minister Narendra Singh Tomar inaugurated Amazon India's Kisan Store. The government handed over sales of fertilizers and seeds to the corporates. The urea that IFFCO sold at Rs 266.50 for a 45 kg bag, was now selling at Rs 199 a kg on Amazon! On Flipkart, the price of 450 grams of urea was listed as Rs 130! This was the shameless black marketing of fertilizers on a platform launched by the Union Agriculture Minister himself!

It was this cynical loot and exploitation by corporate communalism, represented by the Modi-Shah-Ambani-Adani corrupt combine, which was valiantly combated by farmers in this struggle. The Bharat Bandh on 27 September was one of the vital watersheds in this struggle.

24. THE GHASTLY LAKHIMPUR KHERI MASSACRE

It was an incredibly brutal and inhuman attack. Never before since independence had such a thing ever happened.

In a peaceful protest of farmers led by the SKM at Tikunia in Lakhimpur Kheri district of Uttar Pradesh on 3 October 2021, a convoy of vehicles associated with BJP's Union Minister of State for Home Affairs Ajay Mishra Teni, his son Ashish Mishra Teni, and other goons actually mowed down several farmer protestors. Four farmers and one local journalist were killed in this ghastly incident, and several others were seriously injured. A prominent leader of the SKM and the Terai Kisan Sanghatan, Tajinder Singh Virk, was also grievously injured.

Thousands of farmers started assembling on the morning of 3 October in Lakhimpur Kheri district of Uttar Pradesh for a black flag protest against Uttar Pradesh deputy chief minister Keshav Prasad Maurya and Union Minister of State Ajay Mishra Teni, because of the latter's open threat issued against farmer leaders in a public meeting. The farmers with black flags occupied the helipad at Maharaja Agrasen Ground to prevent the deputy CM from landing there. The brutal attack on farmers happened as the farmers were dispersing and leaving the protest site since the deputy CM dropped his plan of coming in a helicopter. Ajay Mishra Teni's son and other goons then drove their cars over the protestors who were on the roads with black flags, and killed five. In a spontaneous and incensed reaction, farmers attacked the BJP goons in one of the cars, and four of them were also killed in the melee that followed.

On the same day, 3 October, in another condemnable development, Haryana chief minister Manohar Lal Khattar was heard in a video clip encouraging BJP-RSS men to pick up lathis and attack farmers, even if this means ending up in jails for a few months! While the farmers' movement had explicitly made peace and non-violence its values, it was clear that the BJP governments acted with murderous intent against their own citizens. SKM condemned the BJP CM's remarks and demanded that he resign from his constitutional post.

A week later, Khattar apologized for his statements inciting violence against farmers. He said he was retracting his statements. He also cancelled his programme in Kaithal since farmers had already announced a protest against his visit.

SERIAL MURDERS OF FARMERS

This was the third serial murder of farmers by the BJP within a month. The first was the murder of Sushil Kajal of Karnal in Haryana on 28 August, as a result of the brutal police lathi charge by the BJP-JJP's Haryana government. The second was the equally brutal killing of two Muslim farmers Saddam Hussain and 12 year-old Sheikh Forid, on 23 September by police firing ordered by the BJP's Assam government. Chief minister Himanta Biswa Sarma was shameless enough to hail the police action. The third is the mowing down of four farmers –Gurvinder Singh (19), Lovepreet Singh (20), Daljeet Singh (35), and Nachattar Singh (60) – and a journalist Raman Kashyap on 3 October in the Lakhimpur Kheri massacre by BJP hoodlums in Uttar Pradesh. The four farmers killed were Sikhs, and the journalist was a Hindu.

Eye witness accounts reveal how the murderous attack was pre-planned, helped by the UP police. It was reported that police removed barricades to allow the vehicles of the Minister's son, who himself was driving the Thar vehicle, to mow down protestors indiscriminately, and the farmers retaliated thereafter. The police helped Ashish Mishra Teni in escaping from the scene. The specific targeting of SKM leader Tajinder Singh Virk was also narrated.

Twelve days later, on Dussehra Day, 15 October, Hannan Mollah, Vijoo Krishnan, P. Krishnaprasad, and I met Tajinder Singh Virk while he was recuperating at Gurgaon after a hospital stay. He had injuries and bandages all over his body. He related to us the horrific incidents at Lakhimpur Kheri in which he miraculously escaped death.

After these brutal and barbaric incidents, there were questions raised by the 'Godi' media and by the notorious BJP-RSS IT cells about the protestors and their violent behaviour. It was only a matter of time before the true narrative of the incidents in Lakhimpur Kheri emerged.

A shocking video emerged on 5 October, which forced even the 'Godi' TV channels of India to demand justice by their standards, even though no media house offered an apology and correction for the false and spurious narrative spun since 3 October. In this video, the explanation given by the Minister Ajay Mishra Teni and his son was proved to be false. The vehicles of the Minister fatally mowed down peacefully walking, unaware protestors who were returning from their protest. Many eyewitness accounts were later released on videos which also revealed that the Minister's son Ashish Mishra was indeed driving the Thar vehicle, from which he later got down and ran away, with support provided by the police. The family of journalist, Raman Kashyap, pointed out that he was also killed by vehicles crushing him.

In an urgently convened virtual press conference, members of the 9-member coordination committee of the SKM addressed the media about the ghastly incidents in Lakhimpur Kheri. The SKM's Richa Singh and Guramneet Mangat who were themselves at Tikunia in Lakhimpur Kheri, also shared the details of the shocking events.

The SKM angrily demanded that the Uttar Pradesh government must immediately impose cases with murder charges under IPC Section 302 against all those involved from the side of Ajay Mishra Teni, and the Union Minister must be dismissed immediately. The SKM also demanded a judicial inquiry by a sitting judge of the Supreme Court.

The Yogi Adityanath-led BJP Uttar Pradesh government tried

numerous ways of preventing people from going to Lakhimpur Kheri, whether it was SKM leaders, social activists, or political leaders. Many SKM leaders were arrested on the way. Section 144 was imposed, and internet services were suspended. The UP government went to the extent of writing to the Punjab government, warning that no person from Punjab would be allowed to enter Lakhimpur Kheri.

The opposition leader and former chief minister of Uttar Pradesh, two sitting chief ministers of Punjab and Chhattisgarh, and a deputy chief minister were also prevented from visiting Lakhimpur Kheri. This showed the panic of the Yogi regime. These incidents showed that the UP government had something to hide, and was protecting the culprits. SKM condemned all these draconian measures of the Uttar Pradesh BJP government.

MASSIVE COUNTRYWIDE PROTESTS

SKM called upon all farmers' organizations across the country to immediately protest at government offices in all districts on 4 October to press for the above demands. SKM appealed to all farmers to continue their protests peacefully and non-violently, as they had done for the past ten months. The movement recognized the various dirty ways in which the BJP-RSS were desperately trying to break unity, and would combat any such attempts.

There were spontaneous protests in response to the massacre in Lakhimpur Kheri from 3 October night, when candlelight marches and rallies were taken out in places like Ambala, Chandigarh, Kurukshetra, and elsewhere. In Puranpur and other places, highways were jammed by protesting farmers. Thousands of farmers poured into Tikunia on 4 October, at the site of the violent incidents, where the bodies of the martyrs were kept.

On 4 and 5 October, large protests were organized at DC/DM offices and other locations in many places across the country.

Reports came in from Bihar, Haryana, Jharkhand, Karnataka, Madhya Pradesh, Maharashtra, Odisha, Punjab, Rajasthan, Telangana, Tamil Nadu, Uttarakhand, Uttar Pradesh, West Bengal, and other states about these protests. A protest organized outside UP Bhawan in New Delhi ended with scores of protestors being picked up and detained for many hours by the Delhi police in Mandir Marg Police Station.

FARMERS FORCE STATE GOVERNMENT TO CONCEDE COMPENSATION

On 4 October an agreement was reached between SKM leaders along with local protesting farmers and families of the deceased, and the state administration, which paved the way for the last rites to be performed of the martyred farmers, after the postmortem. The bodies of the martyrs had been kept in an overnight vigil by thousands of farmers and their families in Tikunia's college ground. The state government would give Rs 45 lakh and a government job each to the families of the farmers who were killed. The injured would be given Rs 10 lakh each. An FIR was registered against Ashish Mishra Teni and 15 others under Sections 302, 120B and other charges, and the government said it would arrest all the accused within a week. A case was registered against Union Minister Ajay Mishra Teni also. The Government agreed to get a retired High Court judge to probe the matter.

Among those SKM leaders who took part in the negotiations with the state government and later addressed the huge condolence meeting in Tikunia were BKU leaders Rakesh Tikait, Dharmendra Malik, and Rajvir Jadaon; AIKS leaders D.P. Singh, Mukut Singh, and Chandrapal Singh; and also Guramneet Mangat, Jagtar Singh Bazwa, and Baba Anup Singh. The huge meeting was attended by thousands of Hindu, Muslim, and Sikh farmers in a spirit of unity.

The agreement with the administration on 4 October was only

to pave the way for the last rites of the martyrs to be performed. The key demands of the SKM remained.

BUTCHER OF LAKHIMPUR KHERI STILL CONTINUES IN UNION CABINET

No worse example of the brazen callousness of the Modi-Shah-led BJP-RSS central government has been witnessed in the last eight years. Months after the inhuman and brutal massacre of farmers at Lakhimpur Kheri, which stunned the nation, the notorious Union Minister of State for Home Affairs, Ajay Mishra Teni, was neither sacked from the Modi cabinet nor was he arrested. He became notorious all over the country as the butcher of Lakhimpur Kheri.

His son Ashish Mishra Teni, along with other BJP goons, actually executed the act of mowing down unsuspecting farmers under their convoy of cars, was also given kid-glove treatment, but with mounting public pressure, was finally arrested. The judicial commission appointed by the BJP state government of Uttar Pradesh was meaningless. This episode shocked the nation and the world and exposed the dirty fascistic, and rank communal nature of the BJP-RSS and their governments at the centre and in Uttar Pradesh.

MAHARASHTRA BANDH CONDEMNS MASSACRE

The Maharashtra Bandh called on 11 October by the ruling MVA, comprising the Shiv Sena, NCP and Congress, to condemn the BJP-incited Lakhimpur Kheri farmers' massacre, was a great success. Left and secular parties and mass fronts and all SKM constituents in the state took part in the Bandh campaign. All activity in the state came to a standstill – public transport, shops, markets, offices, schools, colleges. In hundreds of places, there were road blockades. There was a spontaneous outpouring of grief for the farmer martyrs and anger against the BJP-RSS.

11 October was also the birth anniversary of the renowned freedom fighter, a socialist by convioction, and a leading champion of democracy against the Emergency, Jayaprakash Narayan. The SKM celebrated the anniversary of this great patriot at the Delhi borders and all over the country.

HUGE CONDOLENCE MEETING

On 12 October, to attend the last prayers of the five Lakhimpur Kheri martyrs, tens of thousands of farmers and their supporters reached Tikunia. These were farmers not just from Uttar Pradesh but from all adjoining states. The Uttar Pradesh government tried its best to prevent people from joining the *antim ardaas*. But despite all the obstacles put up by the UP police, people managed to reach Tikunia in massive numbers.

From this prayer meeting in Tikunia, the SKM announced its resolve to secure justice. Among the SKM leaders present in Tikunia on October 12 were Rakesh Tikait, Balbir Singh Rajewal, Darshan Pal, Joginder Singh Ugrahan, Jagjit Singh Dallewal, Gurnam Singh Charuni, Yogendra Yadav, P. Krishnaprasad, Abhimanyu Kohad, Guramneet Mangat, Manjeet Rai, Satyawan, Ashish Mittal, Baldev Singh Nihalgarh, Ruldu Singh Mansa and others. The AIKS in UP was represented by its state president Bharat Singh, state general secretary Mukut Singh, CITU state general secretary Prem Nath Rai, AIDWA state vice president Madhu Garg, and others.

Prayer and homage meetings were held all over the country and thousands of candlelight vigils were held on 12 October to pay respects to the five martyrs and 631 other farmers who were martyred in the current agitation. The sense of outrage among ordinary citizens against the impunity of the BJP Ministers and leaders was palpable everywhere.

INVERTED JUSTICE

The SKM condemned the registering of a case against the farmer leader Tajinder Singh Virk when he was clearly the one who was attacked and seriously injured in Lakhimpur Kheri. Video clips clearly showed that Tajinder Singh Virk was attacked by the 'Thar' vehicle from behind when he was peacefully walking on the road, and later, as he lay bleeding on the road in a dazed state, others were running to help him. Registering an FIR against him was revolting.

Later, two more farmers, Gurvinder Singh and Vichitra Singh, were arrested based on the counter FIR filed by the arrested BJP worker Sumit Jaiswal, who was one of the main accused in the case. These two farmers were sent to police remand. Cases were registered under Sections 147, 323, 324, 336 and 302. It was evident that attempts were being made to frame farmers. The SKM condemned the arrests of the farmers, demanded their release, and reiterated its demand for a Supreme Court-monitored Special Investigation Team (SIT) probe in the case.

The Supreme Court did step in and set up an SIT. The SIT, in its report, concluded that the Lakhimpur Kheri murders were not an accident but were clearly a conspiracy. The Supreme Court pulled up the central government and the UP state government several times. However, within a few months, Ashish Mishra Teni was granted bail by the Allahabad High Court. This was challenged by the SKM in the Supreme Court, which cancelled his bail and he was re-arrested. However, Union Minister Ajay Mishra Teni still remains untouched in the Modi-Shah Raj.

25. BJP LEADERS' EFFIGIES BURNT ON DUSSEHRA

On Dussehra day, 15 October 2021, to mark the triumph of good over evil, effigy-burning of top BJP leaders like Narendra Modi, Amit Shah, Yogi Adityanath, Ajay Mishra Teni, Manohar Lal Khattar, Narendra Singh Tomar, and others took place in thousands of locations all over the country. In Uttar Pradesh, the police took several farmer leaders into preventive detention and house arrests. Despite this, in hundreds of places, the programme was conducted. In Madhya Pradesh, where farmers had assembled, police tried to forcibly prevent them from taking up the effigy burning in some places. In all other states, lakhs of farmers in numerous locations, down to villages, angrily burnt effigies of the BJP leaders, as per the SKM call.

On 18 October, in hundreds of locations across India, protesting farmers occupied railway tracks and platforms. Men and women in, thousands came out for implementing the Rail Roko call of the SKM. More than 290 trains were affected, and more than 40 were cancelled. In Uttar Pradesh, there were many detentions of farmer leaders in numerous places by the police. In Madhya Pradesh, the police arrested protestors in several places, including AIKS joint secretary Badal Saroj and others. In Kacheguda of Telangana also, protestors were arrested. In Kerala, thousands of farmers picketed central government offices all over the state, demanding the dismissal and arrest of Ajay Mishra Teni. Reports of Rail Roko came in from several states.

NATIONWIDE SHAHEED KALASH YATRAS

On 26 October, when the farmers' struggle completed 11 months, large protests were held in hundreds of places all over India to demand the immediate arrest and sacking of Ajay Mishra Teni, the *sutradhaar* of the Lakhimpur Kheri massacre. The protests took various forms including marches, motorcycle rallies, demonstrations, dharnas and so on. At all the six Delhi borders, large public meetings were held. Farmers drove in with tractors into the Meerut Collectorate to protest. Reports came of large actions from several states.

In several states, Shaheed Kalash Yatras were taken out with their ashes to pay homage to the martyrs of the Lakhimpur Kheri massacre. The SKM-led Shaheed Asthikalash Yatras traversed thousands of kilometres across several states and districts in the entire country, and they elicited a massive response from the people. Farmers took vows that they would not allow the martyrs' sacrifice to go in vain and continue the struggle until the demands were secured.

DISTURBING INCIDENT AT SINGHU BORDER

On 15 October, a gruesome murder occurred at Singhu border. The victim and the four accused, who confessed to their crime and were arrested, were all Dalit Sikhs. The accused had clear links with a Nihang group.

The same evening, the SKM issued this statement:

> It has come to the notice of the SKM that a person hailing from Punjab (Lakhbir Singh, son of Darshan Singh, Village Cheema Kalan, Police Station Sarai Amanat Khan, District Tarn Taran) was mutilated and murdered this morning at Singhu border. A Nihang group at the scene has claimed responsibility, saying that the incident took place because of the deceased's attempt to commit sacrilege with regard to the Sarbaloh Granth. The SKM condemns this gruesome killing and wants to make it clear that both the parties to this incident, the Nihang group and the deceased person, have no relation with the SKM. The Morcha is against sacrilege of any religious text or symbol, but that does not give anyone the right to take the law into

their own hands. We demand that the culprits be punished according to law after investigating the allegation of murder and conspiracy.

On 16 October, in its press release, the SKM stated, 'SKM demands an investigation into the allegation of conspiracy to sabotage the movement through sacrilege and promotion of disturbance by hurting religious sentiments. From media reports from the victim's village and family, it appears that he had been receiving mysterious calls which he would take in secrecy. Victim Lakhbir Singh is supposed to have told his sister that 'his reach has increased now and has gone far'. All this points to a deep conspiracy of some sort, as SKM has been pointing out.'

The conspiracy angle was further confirmed with a report that appeared on 19 October in *The Tribune*. It said, 'Baba Aman Singh, who heads one of the Nihang sects, and a Sikh group based in Onatrio, Canada, may have had a role in the behind-the-scene efforts by the government to end the farmers' stir.' The report further says that Baba Aman Singh attended a meeting with Union Agriculture Minister Narendra Singh Tomar for this purpose. Along with this report, *The Tribune* has printed a telling photograph showing Baba Aman Singh, a dismissed cop and murder convict Gurmeet 'Pinki', Narendra Singh Tomar, and BJP Kisan Morcha leader Sukhminderpal Singh Grewal together! The cat was now out of the bag.

26. INDIA SLIPS IN WORLD HUNGER INDEX

On 16 October, World Food Day, India slipped further in global hunger ranking, from 94 out of 107 countries in 2020, to 101 out of 116 countries in 2021, despite boasting about record production of food grains, milk, fruits, vegetables, fisheries and so on. The widespread incidence of hunger and malnutrition could not be denied. The overflowing public granaries did not reach the needy. The fact that India's food security basket, assured under the PDS, had not been diversified to deliver proper nutrition was disastrous for both farmers and consumers.

The corporatization paradigm being promoted in our food and farming systems, represented by the three anti-farmer laws and other policies, would prove even more disastrous, and that is what the farmers' movement fought against. In its pushback against corporate control over our food and farming systems, this movement was trying to establish equity, viability, sustainability, and nutrition security. Within this pushback are issues of skewed cropping, so-called 'fortification' of food to allow more corporate takeover of our food, de-regulation of food stock-piling and freedom to black-market, dismantling of PDS, trade liberalization allowing the dumping of foreign produce into our markets, destruction of forests, diversion of rice to ethanol production, and several such reductionist non-solutions.

FARMER SUICIDES INCREASE

The Government of India's National Crime Records Bureau (NCRB) pegged the annual number of farmer deaths by suicide in 2020 at 10,677. 5,579 of these deaths were of cultivators and 5,098 were of agricultural labourers, as per the NCRB annual report on Accidental Deaths and Suicides in India, for 2020. Maharashtra, Karnataka, Andhra Pradesh, Madhya Pradesh and

Chhattisgarh accounted for the largest number of farmer deaths by suicide in 2020. While there is an increase in the number of farmer deaths by suicide compared to 2019, several critiques exist of the reliability of this data in NCRB reports, and there has been a trend of reporting declining farmer deaths by suicide since 2016. The anomaly of several states like TMC-ruled West Bengal reporting zero farmer deaths by suicide in these reports is notorious. While this suppression of the real picture with regard to farmer deaths by suicide is on, there is no denying the acute distress that farmers are going through, with the lockdown-induced hardships adding to the same. SKM demanded once again that the Government of India does not exacerbate the situation of farmers further by bringing in pro-corporate laws that worsen the situation for farmers.

UNSEASONAL RAINS HIT FARMERS HARD

In October 2021, heavy unseasonal rains in several parts of the country destroyed the effort put in by lakhs of farmers in different states. Thousands of hectares of paddy and other crops lay destroyed in Uttar Pradesh, Uttarakhand, Haryana, Punjab, and other states. It was estimated that 120 lakh metric tonnes of standing paddy crop ready to be harvested had been affected by rains and hailstorms. Paddy brought to market yards was lying in yards full of water. The disaster compensation given through NDRF and SDRF mechanisms was meagre and did not cover the losses incurred by farmers during such natural disasters. The PMFBY, as we saw earlier, had become a bogus scheme.

SKM demanded that that the governments take up a comprehensive assessment of the damage faced by farmers and pay them compensation and crop insurance benefits immediately. Farmers were also agitating for compensation for cotton crop damage due to pink bollworm, and for paddy procurement to be started in right earnest in several locations.

FERTILISER SHORTAGES AND BLACK MARKETING

News about severe hardships in accessing chemical fertilizers such as DAP continued to pour in from various parts, including deaths while standing in long queues or even farmer deaths by suicide. The fertilizer shortage reflected not only the lack of planning and management by the Government of India but also its encouragement to black marketing. The Government's claims that it had created a safety net for market fluctuations after the pandemic lay exposed.

The hard-hitting AIKS press release on this issue stated,

> Over the last three decades, with continuous undermining of the public sector and domestic capacity for manufacturing fertilizers, India has become increasingly dependent on imports of fertilizers. In 2020, of the total supply, 25 per cent of Urea, 68 per cent of DAP and 100 per cent of Potash was imported. Even for fertilizer that is manufactured in India, key raw materials such as phosphatic rock and phosphoric acid are imported.
>
> More seriously, Government of India did not do anything to ensure that adequate fertilizer stocks were obtained before the Rabi sowing. Total supply (production and import) of DAP between March and September in 2021 has been 31 per cent lower than in the same months last year. The supply of Potash in the same months has been 68 per cent lower than last year. The fall in supply of fertilizer has also been accompanied with an increase in prices as no further increase in subsidy or a policy of price regulation has been announced by the government.
>
> Under the privatized and deregulated regime, large scale hoarding and black marketing of fertilizers is going on. On the other hand, farmers are unable to get fertilizers even after standing in long queues for days. It is reported that five

farmers died in the Bundelkhand region in Uttar Pradesh due to exhaustion while standing in line for two to three days. One farmer in Uttar Pradesh and another in Madhya Pradesh are reported to have died by suicide as they had taken loans but were not getting fertilizers. Unless immediate corrective steps are taken it could have serious consequences for the peasantry and agriculture as a whole.

AIKS demands that the central government should immediately constitute a high-level task force to explore the possible ways to immediately secure adequate supplies of fertilizers, re-introduce price controls for all fertilizers under the NBS scheme, and establish a high-level committee of experts to prepare a roadmap for enhancing the national production of fertilizers and preparing a mechanism to ensure that adequate stocks of fertilizers are maintained.

FARMERS VINDICATED IN STUBBLE BURNING CASE

In an important hearing in November on Delhi's air pollution crisis, the Government of India made a critical disclosure – it stated that farm residue burning contributed only 10 per cent of the emissions, on an annual average. This is obviously lower than even the low 25 per cent mentioned by the CJI-led Bench in the last hearing, where the Court observed that farmer-bashing had become a fashion now and that stubble burning was not the only reason for pollution. It asked the petitioners and others to stop blaming farmers for the crisis, saying that most of the pollution was from vehicular pollution, firecracker burning and dust. The Government's disclosure prompted the Supreme Court to once again say that the hue and cry over farm fires is without any basis. 'The farmers' stubble burning contributes to 4 per cent of the pollution and we are targeting something insignificant', said the CJI-led Bench.

The SKM and protesting farmers had always pointed out that

farmers were being unfairly blamed for Delhi's air quality crisis, and further, targeting farmers was not a solution to the problem. SKM and the protesting farmers stood vindicated by the Supreme Court's observations since the movement had been asking that farmers should not be blamed for Delhi's air pollution problems. Despite promising the protesting farmers that the statute related to the Delhi Air Quality Commission would remove penal provisions applicable to farmers, the Modi Government deviously brought in a new Section 15 that would enable the Delhi Air Quality Commission to target farmers if it chooses to, in future. SKM demanded, again, that this new Section 15 be deleted from the statute immediately.

NATIONAL CONVENTION OF WORKERS

On 11 November, a National Convention of Workers was organized by the CTUs and Independent Federations at Jantar Mantar in Delhi. This Convention highlighted the anti-worker, anti-farmer, anti-people and anti-national policies of the BJP-NDA government, called for strengthening worker-peasant unity in the countrywide mass actions on 26 November, for a massive two-day All India Strike during the Budget Session of Parliament, and for intensifying the united struggles of both workers and farmers. An SKM delegation was invited and took part in it.

TRIBUTE TO MARTYRS OF OUR FREEDOM STRUGGLE

On 15 November, Adivasi freedom fighter and martyr Birsa Munda's birth anniversary was observed all over the country. At a time when the Government of India is contemplating amendments in the Forest Conservation Act 1980 that will favour the corporates and be detrimental to the rights of Adivasis and their livelihoods, tribute was paid to Birsa Munda.

On 16 November, the martyrdom day was observed of Sardar Kartar Singh Sarabha and Vishnu Ganesh Pingale of the heroic Ghadar Party that fought against British rule and oppression in India. Both were hanged to death in the Lahore Central Jail on 16 November 1915, on charges of conspiracy. Sarabha was only 19, and Pingale was 27. Sarabha was an inspiration for Shaheed Bhagat Singh. On the same day, the martyrdom day of Veerangana Uda Devi Pasi was also marked with respect. She was a Dalit warrior in the First War of Independence in 1857, and fought valiantly in the Battle of Sikandar Bagh against the British.

PROTEST AGAINST NARENDRA MODI IN GLASGOW

A large number of Indian diaspora in the United Kingdom, who were supporters of the farmers' movement, gathered in Glasgow to protest against Prime Minister Narendra Modi. Holding placards that said 'Struggle of Indian Farmers is Our Struggle' and with banners that called Modi a 'killer of hundreds of innocent protestors', these people of Indian origin extended their support to the protesting farmers. The protestors held up banners saying that Modi was not welcome in Scotland. The protest happened at a time when Modi was visiting Glasgow to take part in the United Nations' COP26 summit, to tackle the global warming emergency on an urgent and committed basis by all countries of the world.

BJP SUFFERS SETBACKS IN BY-ELECTIONS

The Lok Sabha and Vidhan Sabha bypoll results that were declared on 2 November resulted in a big setback to the BJP, especially in Haryana, Himachal Pradesh and Rajasthan, the very states where the farmers' struggle had been continuing for a year. This held a clue to what is in store for the BJP, if it does not align government policies with citizens' interests, said SKM.

The BJP secured only one out of three seats in the Parliamentary by-elections. In 14 states, assembly by-elections took place on 30 seats. In states like Haryana, Himachal Pradesh and Rajasthan, where the farmers' movement had urged voters to punish BJP for its anti-farmer policies, the results went against the BJP. It lost one parliamentary and three assembly seats in Himachal Pradesh, and one assembly seat each in Haryana and Rajasthan.

27. WOMEN AND YOUTH IN THE STRUGGLE

One of the most remarkable features of this farmers' struggle was the role played in it by women and youth throughout the one year that it lasted. Women and youth truly strengthened and steeled the struggle in every way. Tens of thousands of them thronged all the Delhi borders month after month, braving the innumerable difficulties that came their way. In the struggle that was spread out all over the country, too, they played a stellar role.

THE REMARKABLE ROLE OF WOMEN

In recent times, women had played a leading role in the anti-CAA struggle across the country in 2019. The Shaheen Bagh saga in Delhi, and the countless Shaheen Baghs in every nook and corner of the country, were led courageously and consistently by tens of thousands of women.

Similarly, in this year-long farmers' struggle, women took part in even larger numbers. At a time when the communal and regressive forces want to push women back to the boundary walls of their homes, women scuttled their plans and made their homes under the open sky, facing biting cold, scorching heat and torrential rains.

Despite historically being the world's first farmers, women have had to struggle at every step to be recognized as farmers. When women do 75 per cent of the work in the fields, why is it that they do not get the identity of being farmers, they rightly asked. In this movement, women through their mass participation, staked their claim to being farmers very effectively. They brought to the centre of discussion the work of women in agriculture, the impact of policies related to them, and the disastrous effect of the Farm Laws on them. The next crucial battle for women is undoubtedly to claim and get ownership rights on the land that they cultivate.

Women had always worked shoulder to shoulder with men on the farms. But now they also played the same role in the movement. From elderly women to young girls, women of all ages participated in the movement in tens of thousands. Not only peasant women, but also working class women and even middle class women supported the struggle. The large participation of women made a major contribution in making the movement disciplined and peaceful.

Women not only took care of the farm and the home, but they also took part in local movements at the various toll plazas. They provided services to the langars at the borders. For a whole year, the struggle became a part of their daily lives. Every day they heard new things through speeches, songs and political discussions.

And then they came forward boldly to speak. They wrote and sang songs. They conducted the various stages on the borders. They became part of the Mahila Kisan Samitis and of the farmers' organizations. They moved ahead by breaking the conservative fabric of society.

The SKM took particular care to highlight the role of women in this farmers' struggle. It gave a call for observing 3 January as the birth anniversary of the pioneering social reformer Savitribai Phule, who, way back in 1848, had set up the first girls' school in India at Pune. Several organizations like AIDWA, AIPWA, NFIW, and joint forums like Hum Agar Utthe Nahin Toh (If We Do Not Rise) celebrated the day at all the six Delhi borders and throughout the country.

On 18 January, Mahila Kisan Day was widely observed at the six Delhi borders and across the length and breadth of the country. This call of the SKM acknowledged the lion's share of women in agricultural operations.

The SKM then gave a call to celebrate 8 March as International Women's Day. Women's organizations and groups all over the world have celebrated this day for several decades. This year, they mobilized tens of thousands of women in these programmes all over India.

Two days in the SKM Kisan Parliament – 26 July and 9 August – were run entirely by women. They were the Mahila Kisan Sansads. On 9 August, it was the women in the Kisan Sansad who passed the no-confidence motion against the Modi-led BJP-RSS government.

THE ENTHUSIASTIC ROLE OF YOUTH

Youth also took part in the struggle in their tens of thousands, not only at the Delhi borders, but also all over the country. Full of energy and determination, they infused vigour and enthusiasm in the struggle. With the immortal Bhagat Singh as their icon, they rose against injustice of all kinds.

Another remarkable contribution of the peasant youth was the wide propagation of the farmers' struggle through social media, over which they had varying degrees of mastery. It was they who prepared and popularized the numerous effective slogans of the struggle. It was they who made attractive and meaningful posters that appealed to the general public and involved it in struggle in various ways. It was they who provided the backbone for the large protest actions all over the country, in which peasants and workers of all ages joined.

There is no doubt at all that the whole-hearted participation and the leadership of women and youth in this struggle helped to make it stronger, deeper and richer in every way.

28. EPIC VICTORY OVER CORPORATE COMMUNALISM

It was an epic victory of the one year-long struggle of the farmers of India over corporate communalism, as represented by the Modi-Shah-led BJP-RSS central government and its alliance with foreign and domestic corporates, represented by the two ace crony corporates Ambani and Adani. Prime Minister Narendra Modi's nationally televized address to the country on November 19, 2021 to coincide with the Guru Nanak Jayanti, agreeing to repeal all the three hated Farm Laws, was a stinging defeat for all of them. It was a resounding victory not only for the farmers of India, but for democracy itself. And it will long be remembered in history.

This was only the second time in the last eight years of his rule that Modi had been forced to make a humiliating climbdown. The first was in 2015, when he was forced to take back the Land Acquisition Act Amendment Ordinance, again as a result of a countrywide farmers' struggle.

There was tremendous and spontaneous jubilation not only at the Delhi borders of the farmers' struggle, but among farmers, workers and the people all over the country, at this great victory. Crackers were burst, sweets were distributed, and a carnival atmosphere prevailed. There was a feeling of great jubilation that a unique people's struggle had humbled a tyrannical regime.

This valiant farmers' struggle under the leadership of the SKM had braved every kind of repression and defamation from the RSS-BJP regime. It had also surmounted the deadly Covid pandemic. It was completely united, peaceful and democratic. It was also completely secular, with lakhs of peasant participants cutting across religion, caste, region and language. It was concentrated at the Delhi borders, but it had spread all over the country. It was fully supported by the working class and agricultural labourers, and by all other sections like women, youth and students. These were the reasons why it could not be crushed.

WHY THIS SUDDEN VOLTE FACE?

Although the PM's sudden announcement of repealing the Farm Laws was surprising, it was clear in recent months that the central government was being thrown increasingly on the defensive by the farmers' struggle. This was the result of five major factors.

The *first* was the massive one million strong SKM-organized Kisan Mazdoor Mahapanchayat at Muzaffarnagar on 5 September 2021. The farmers and workers came in huge numbers mostly from Uttar Pradesh, but large contingents also came from Uttarakhand, Punjab, Haryana, Rajasthan and Madhya Pradesh. Its most distinctive feature was that it succeeded in rebuilding secular unity, which had been seriously disrupted by the RSS-BJP-VHP in the Muzaffarnagar communal riots in 2013. The country had not seen such a mammoth rally in recent years.

The *second* was the unprecedented success of the Bharat Bandh call given by the SKM on 27 September. This was the third Bharat Bandh call in the one year long farmers' struggle, and the most successful of all three. Millions of farmers, workers, agricultural labourers, middle class employees, traders, women, youth and students from all over India, came out on the streets to make it a magnificent and unprecedented success.

The *third* was the increasing tempo of the struggle in Uttar Pradesh, Punjab and Haryana. In Punjab, the farmers' struggle had gone down to practically every home in the state. The constant repression by the BJP-JJP state government in Haryana, and the valiant and victorious fightback by the farmers, was a saga in itself. The struggle was also spreading in Uttar Pradesh.

The *fourth* was the stunning and dastardly Lakhimpur Kheri

massacre in Uttar Pradesh of four farmers and a journalist. Along with this was the protection given by the Prime Minister, Home Minister and UP Chief Minister to the heinous culprits. This created great revulsion among people. On Dussehra Day, October 15, effigies of top BJP leaders were burnt in thousands of places all over the country by lakhs of farmers and workers. On 18 October, Rail Roko stirs were conducted in hundreds of places. The Asthi Kalash Yatras of the Lakhimpur Kheri martyrs travelled all over the country and drew massive response everywhere.

And the *fifth* and most important factor was, of course, the impending state assembly elections in Uttar Pradesh, Uttarakhand and Punjab. There was fear in ruling circles of the deepening alienation of the people in the sensitive border state of Punjab, which had a few decades ago been the victim of violent separatism. The results of the November by-elections saw a rout of the BJP in Himachal, Haryana and Rajasthan, the frontline states of the farmers' struggle. The RSS-BJP belatedly realized the grave danger that they faced in the impending elections.

The announcement of the repeal of the Farm Laws was a cumulative result of these five immediate factors, apart from the year-long epic saga of the united farmers' struggle itself.

However, the government's announcement of repeal was a classic case of too little, too late. 715 farmers had been martyred in this struggle over the last one year. The responsibility for this terrible human cost lay squarely with the Modi Government. Five of them were murdered in cold blood at Lakhimpur Kheri by Modi's lieutenant in the central cabinet Ajay Mishra Teni, and he still roamed about scot free! This would be unthinkable in any democracy.

Also, repeal of the Farm Laws was certainly the main demand of this struggle. But there were also other key demands which were not addressed by the Prime Minister or the Government.

The first meeting of the SKM after the PM's announcement was held amidst great enthusiasm on 21 November at Singhu border.

There was jubilation that one part of the battle had been won. But there was also determination to see that the other just demands of this struggle were conceded. The two major decisions taken were: First, sending an open letter to the PM listing out the major pending demands of the farmers and demanding a resolution of those issues through talks. Second, continuing all the pre-decided programmes of the struggle.

LARGE MAHAPANCHAYAT AT LUCKNOW

Accordingly, on 22 November, a massive Kisan Mazdoor Mahapanchayat of tens of thousands of peasants was held at Lucknow, the capital of Uttar Pradesh. Women came in large numbers. The mood was infectious – of both victory and determination. The rally echoed the resolve of the SKM to continue the struggle until the pending demands were met. It also warned against the communal conspiracies of the RSS-BJP and called for the defeat of the BJP in the coming state assembly elections in Uttar Pradesh, Uttarakhand and Punjab.

The Lucknow rally was addressed by SKM leaders Rakesh Tikait, Darshan Pal, Joginder Singh Ugrahan, Hannan Mollah, Jagmohan Singh, Yogendra Yadav, Atul Kumar Anjan, Ashish Mittal, myself, and many others. BKU (Tikait) leader Dharmendra Malik and AIKS UP state general secretary Mukut Singh conducted the meeting. AIKS joint secretaries P. Krishnaprasad and Badal Saroj were present, along with the UP state leadership. The strength of the AIKS and AIAWU in the Lucknow rally, just as in the earlier Muzaffarnagar rally, was excellent. Hundreds of AIKS flags and hoardings adorned the area surrounding the rally in Lucknow.

THE SIGNIFICANCE OF THE VICTORY

On 26 November 2021, the farm movement completed one

year of its epic struggle, with lakhs of farmers, joined by workers, agricultural labourers, women, youth, students and common citizens, in nationwide actions. It was also the first anniversary of the All India Strike of the working class. November 26 is also observed as the Constitution Day of India. On this day, in the year 1949, the Constitution was adopted by the Constituent Assembly. Our founding fathers fought a long-drawn battle against the repressive British regime, which sought to destroy India, its people and their livelihoods for the gain of one company.

The day will forever be remembered as one of the greatest moments of a people's struggle in history. This day marked twelve long months of the farmers struggle, with numerous setbacks but also great victories which seemed unlikely, and even impossible, and with a determination to continue to fight for the unfulfilled demands of the farmers. The farmers' movement stood as a testimony to the will of the common people to fight against a tyrannical government, and it will be remembered as such for a long, long time to come.

The struggle also drew strength from its alliance with trade unions, and other progressive and democratic mass organizations including women, student and youth organizations. Nearly all opposition political parties of India stood in support of the farmers in the year-long struggle. Numerous sections of society including artists, academics, writers, doctors, lawyers etc contributed their part to this people's movement. The SKM expresseed its deep appreciation to all the participants and supporters of this movement, and reiterated that the repeal of the three anti-farmer, anti-people and pro-corporate Farm Laws was only the first major victory.

The fact that such a long struggle had to continue for more than a year was itself a stark reflection on the utter insensitivity and callous arrogance of India's BJP-RSS government towards its toiling citizens. Over the course of twelve months of one of the largest and longest protest movements across the world and in history, millions of people took part in the struggle which spread to almost every state, every district and every tehsil of India.

Apart from the repeal of the three hated Farm Laws, the movement achieved several victories for farmers, common citizens and the nation at large. It created a sense of unified identity for the farmers, cutting across regional, religious or caste divisions. Farmers discovered a newfound sense of dignity and pride in their identity as farmers, and their assertion as citizens. This struggle deepened the roots of democracy and secularism.

Large demonstrations of victory, solidarity and support for the farmers' movement came from the Indian diaspora, supported by thousands of people abroad. Impressive rallies were held on November 26 at several places in the USA, UK, Canada, France, Australia, New Zealand and other countries in Europe.

Numerous international organizations lent their solidarity to the movement. A letter of support was issued by the international farmers' organization La Via Campesina. It said, 'India's farmers have inspired the world with their resilience. They have shown us what a united struggle of the working class and the peasantry can achieve even in the face of all adversities. Over the last year, this protest has stitched alliances with workers' unions and other social movements and issued inspiring messages of solidarity, communal harmony and unity among rural societies.'

History was made on 29 November 2021, when the BJP-RSS central government was forced to repeal the hated Farm Laws in Parliament. However, this was done in typical Modi style, without an iota of grace, truth, or democracy. No debate was allowed on the Bill tabled to repeal the three laws. Consequently, the repeal took only four minutes.

29. THE LAST MAHAPANCHAYAT IN MUMBAI

The last massive statewide Kisan Mazdoor Mahapanchayat in this farmers' struggle was held on 28 November 2021 at Azad Maidan in Mumbai, on the occasion of the death anniversary of Mahatma Jotirao Phule. Tens of thousands of peasants, workers, agricultural labourers, women, youth and students of all religions and castes from all over Maharashtra thronged it.

It was organized by the Samyukta Shetkari Kamgar Morcha (SSKM), which comprises around 100 organizations of peasants, workers, agricultural workers, women, youth and students. There were large contingents from the districts of Palghar, Thane, Nashik, Raigad, Ahmednagar, Dhule, Nandurbar, Jalgaon and Mumbai itself. Several organizations had put in great efforts and had mobilized well. The AIKS strength was by far the largest.

The Mahapanchayat was presided over by J.P. Gavit, ex-MLA from the AIKS and Milind Ranade from NTUI. It was addressed by SKM national leaders Ashish Mittal, Atul Kumar Anjaan, B. Venkat, Darshan Pal, ex-MP Hannan Mollah, Jasbir Kaur Nat, Medha Patkar, Pratibha Shinde, Rajaram Singh, Rakesh Tikait, Tajinder Singh Virk, Yogendra Yadav, Yudhvir Singh, and myself; and also by SSKM state leaders Dr Ajit Nawale, Devanand Pawar, Feroze Mithiborwala, MLC Jayant Patil, Kishor Dhamale, Madhu Dhodi, Namdev Gavade, ex-MLA Narasayya Adam, Rajendra Bawake, Raju Korde, Shyam Kale, Ulka Mahajan, ex- MLC Vidya Chavan, and Vishal Hiwale.

At the end, as AIKS President, I moved a condolence resolution for all the 715 martyrs of this farmers' struggle, and tens of thousands of participants stood up to pay homage. The Mahapanchayat concluded with the National Anthem.

The galaxy of national and state leaders of various farmers' and workers' organizations hailed the victory of the year-long farmers' struggle over the BJP-RSS government and its corporate allies in getting the Farm Laws repealed, and also declared their determination to fight for the remaining demands.

All the leaders led a broadside attack against the anti-people, pro-corporate, communal and authoritarian BJP-RSS government and called for the defeat of the BJP in the coming state assembly elections and also in the ensuing statewide local body elections in Maharashtra.

Leaders also demanded that the MVA Maharashtra state government drop the three farm bills tabled in the last state assembly session. These had been strongly opposed by the SSKM because they mimicked the three Central Farm Laws with some minor amendments. With the repeal of the three Farm Laws, these three Farm Bills must also be withdrawn. The MVA state government subsequently withdrew them in its cabinet meeting on 15 December. Some speakers also demanded an honourable settlement for the one lakh State Transport bus workers who had been striking for their legitimate demands; stringent implementation of the Forest Rights Act (FRA); raising the price paid to farmers for milk, soybean, and cotton; and ensuring compensation to farmers, whose crops had been destroyed by unseasonal rains, under the Prime Minister Fasal Bima Yojana (PMFBY).

All the Sikh Gurudwaras of New Mumbai came together and provided free lunch, breakfast and tea at Azad Maidan to all the participants. They were warmly thanked and applauded.

CULMINATION OF THE SHAHEED KALASH YATRAS

This Mahapanchayat marked the culmination of the SSKM-led Shaheed Kalash Yatras of the Lakhimpur Kheri martyrs that began on 27 October from Mahatma Jotirao Phule and Savitribai Phule's historic house in Pune, which has been declared as a national monument. Mahatma Phule was a champion of the peasantry, an inveterate opponent of the caste system and women's oppression, and the author of seminal works like Slavery and The Whipcord of the Cultivator. His wife, Savitribai Phule, was also a great social reformer and the founder of the first girls' school in India at Pune in 1848. The Shaheed Kalash Yatras traversed hundreds of villages across thirty districts of the state, and they converged in Mumbai on 27 November.

On 27 November, the Shaheed Kalash Yatra paid tribute to the statue of Chhatrapati Shivaji, whom Mahatma Phule had described as the 'King of the Peasantry'; the Chaitya Bhoomi of Dr Babasaheb Ambedkar, a champion of the struggle against caste and gender oppression and one of the main architects of the Constitution of India; the memorial to Shaheed Babu Genu, a peasant turned textile mill worker who was crushed in Mumbai on 12 December 1930 by a British truck when he was protesting against British cloth; and the statue of Mahatma Gandhi, the towering leader of the freedom struggle against British imperialism and a champion of truth, non-violence and secularism – values that had guided the farmers' struggle.

On the morning of 28 November, the Shaheed Kalash Yatra paid homage at the Hutatma Chowk, which commemorates the 106 martyrs of the iconic Samyukta Maharashtra Movement in the 1950s. The ashes of the martyrs were immersed in the Arabian Sea off the Gateway of India in a special programme through boats, in the evening after the Mahapanchayat.

On 29 November, the very next day after the Mumbai Mahapanchayat, the three hated Farm Laws were finally repealed by both Houses of Parliament. On 2 December, the President of India gave his assent to the Farm Laws Repeal Bill. A Gazette Notification was issued to give effect to the repeal. With this, one crucial battle ended in victory.

30. A HISTORIC BATTLE WON, BUT WAR WILL CONTINUE

On 4 December 2021, the Samyukta Kisan Morcha (SKM) held an important meeting to discuss the pending demands of the farmers' movement and the lack of a formal response from the Government of India. It was decided unanimously that the farmers' agitation will continue, until formal and satisfactory responses are obtained from the Government of India. The SKM had sent an open letter to the Prime Minister on 21 November, two days after the Prime Minister's address to the nation to announce the repeal of the three farm laws on 19 November.

SKM STANDS FIRM ON PENDING DEMANDS

The Government of India however chose to dither in responding to some of the other issues that were raised by the protesting farmers. 'Farm unions of India have a bitter experience from the past of securing only oral assurances and ending their agitation and finding that governments renege on their meagre oral assurances too. We will not end this agitation without formal responses on each of the pending issues being raised by us', said the SKM.

After the 4 December meeting, the SKM issued the following press release:

> SKM formed a five-member Committee consisting of Ashok Dhawale, Balbir Singh Rajewal, Gurnam Singh Charuni, Shiv Kumar Sharma 'Kakkaji' and Yudhvir Singh to negotiate with the Government of India for resolving the pending issues. There were six pending demands of the farmers – a legal entitlement for all farmers to realize remunerative MSP

for any agricultural produce that they sell; withdrawal of Electricity Amendments Bill 2020/2021; deletion of Section 15 in the law related to setting up of a Commission for Delhi Air Quality regulation; and three issues that have arisen as part of the ongoing struggle – withdrawal of thousands of cases foisted on protesting farmers and their supporters in various states including Delhi, Haryana, Uttar Pradesh, Uttarakhand, Himachal Pradesh, Madhya Pradesh, Chandigarh, Rajasthan etc.; rehabilitation for the kin of the 715 martyrs of the movement; land allotment for a memorial to be built for them; and arrest and sacking of Ajay Mishra Teni for justice in the Lakhimpur Kheri farmers' massacre.

The next meeting of SKM was fixed for 7 December, with two days kept for the Government of India to respond to the SKM and work along with the five-member committee to take this agitation to its logical conclusion. On 7 December, for the first time in this year-long struggle, the SKM received a serious written draft proposal from the Government of India. The proposal was constructively discussed by farmer leaders at the SKM meeting the same day at Singhu border. The five-member committee presided over this meeting. It was decided that the Morcha would send concrete amendments to the Government's proposal and would reconvene at 2 pm on 8 December for further discussion.

GOVERNMENT RELENTS

On 8 December, the five member committee held its meeting followed by a press conference at the AIKS central office in New Delhi. After hard bargaining by the SKM, the government sent a revised draft which was placed before the SKM meeting on the afternoon of December 8. It was only when it was democratically and unanimously approved by all SKM leaders that it was sent back to the government for finalization.

On the morning of 9 December, the government sent its official signed letter to the SKM, which was placed and approved in a massive SKM meeting at Singhu border amidst tremendous enthusiasm.

The letter sent to the SKM from Mr Sanjay Agarwal, Secretary, Ministry of Agriculture and Farmers Welfare, Government of India, stated as follows:

> Keeping in view the demands raised by the ongoing farmers protests, and with the motivation of finding an amicable resolution, following are the Government of India's proposals:
> 1. Hon. Prime Minister as well as Hon. Agriculture Minister have already announced the constitution of a committee on the MSP issue. The committee will include representatives of the central government, state governments, farmer organizations and agricultural scientists. It is here clarified that the committee will also include SKM representatives. One of the mandates of the committee will be to find a way to ensure MSP for farmers across the country. The government has already previously assured that the present levels of procurement at MSP will continue all over the country.
> 2. With regards to the police cases put on farmers in the course of the movement, Uttar Pradesh, Uttarakhand, Himachal Pradesh, Madhya Pradesh and Haryana state governments have agreed that the protest related cases will be withdrawn with immediate effect.
> 2a. All cases related to the farmer protests registered against farmers and their supporters by the Government of India and its related agencies, in Delhi and other union territories, will be withdrawn with immediate effect. The Government of India will also appeal to other state governments to take steps to withdraw cases related to the farmers' protests.
> 3. The Haryana and Uttar Pradesh governments have principally agreed to provide compensation to farmers who

died during the course of the movement. On points 2 & 3, the Punjab government has already issued public statements.

4. Consultations will be held with all stakeholders/SKM on the clauses related to farmers in the draft Electricity (Amendment) Bill. The Bill will be placed in the Parliament only after thorough discussions with the SKM.

5. Farmers have been freed from all criminal liabilities for stubble burning in section 14 & 15 of the law passed by the Union government.

SKM HAILS VICTORY

The important last SKM press release of the farmers' struggle on 9 December 2021 is given below:

> The Government of India, through the Secretary, Ministry of Agriculture & Farmers' Welfare, sends a formal letter to Samyukta Kisan Morcha agreeing to several pending demands of the protesting farmers – Samyukta Kisan Morcha formally announces the lifting of the morchas at the Delhi Borders on national highways and various other locations in response – Current agitation stands suspended – Battle has been won and the war to ensure farmers' rights, especially to secure MSP as a legal entitlement for all farmers, will continue: SKM.
>
> SKM dedicates the fabulous and historic victory of this struggle to around 715 martyrs of the movement, including those in Lakhimpur Kheri – SKM congratulates all the protesting farmers and citizens, and their supporters wholeheartedly for waging an unprecedented struggle and for the gains of the movement.
>
> Farmers' unity, peace and patience have been the key to the victory and these will not be allowed to erode in any circumstance, vow the farmers – SKM decides collectively to stay alert and ensure that promises are kept.

Considering that the nation is mourning the demise of the Chief of Defence Staff Mr Bipin Rawat and his associates, SKM decides to postpone all celebrations with regard to the victory of farmers, and celebratory rallies will be taken out day after tomorrow (11 December), when farmers leave the morcha sites together in victory rallies.

To ensure that the GOI keeps to its commitments made to the protesting farmers, and to chart out the future course of action, SKM will hold its next meeting on 15 January in Delhi.

SKM thanks local communities at morcha sites profusely for their patience and support throughout the long agitation, and apologizes to them for the inconveniences caused to them – SKM also thanks trade unions, women's organizations and youth/student outfits who struggled along with farmers in this agitation, lawyers who extended legal aid and solidarity, doctors who set up medical camps and gave their untiring services, various religious bodies that set up langars and fed the protestors unconditionally and uninterruptedly, various progressive organizations that stood in support including human rights groups, numerous artists who were there constantly with the movement, numerous organizations that continuously and consistently responded to SKM calls for action, highway dhaba owners and people who gave space for the Kisan Andolan to run its organizational meetings, NRIs and international farmers' organizations and others who took up solidarity actions in their own locations, hundreds of volunteers who participated by giving their sewa and many others including well wishers.

All these decisions were conveyed in a widely attended media conference on 9 December at the Singhu border by SKM leaders Balbir Singh Rajewal, Darshan Pal, Gurnam Singh Charuni, Hannan Mollah, Rakesh Tikait, Shivkumar Sharma 'Kakkaji', Yogendra Yadav, and myself.

The CITU, AIKS, AIAWU, AIDWA, DYFI and SFI in a joint statement, said, 'The historic victory of the farmers' struggle marks the success of democracy over the corporate driven authoritarian and communal forces that dictate the Modi Government. This great victory of the peasantry and working class over the corporate and neoliberal forces will further strengthen democracy, secularism and the plural culture of India. This will also strengthen the struggles of various sections of the society against the neoliberal policies.'

The Joint Platform of Central Trade Unions in its statement, said, 'We, the trade unions, will stand vigil along with the SKM, while carrying on the agitation for the rights of the toiling people, including the forthcoming all India strike on 28-29 March 2022 against the complete sell out of our national wealth and the atrocious onslaught on the rights and cruelest exploitation of the working people being carried out by the corporate-servile government at the centre. We consider Worker-Peasant Unity as the priceless achievement of this epic struggle.'

11 December 2021 marked the day when an epic one year long battle of the farmers of India ended in a magnificent victory. Peasants and workers celebrated this sweet victory for over a week from 9 December, and particularly on 11 December, which was designated as the Nationwide Victory Day by the SKM.

Tens of thousands of farmers who had stayed at the Delhi borders for over a year since 26 November 2020 started returning to their homes in Punjab, Haryana, Madhya Pradesh, Rajasthan, Uttar Pradesh, and Uttarakhand. They received a resounding welcome everywhere with sweets and flowers. The victory of the farmers' struggle instilled confidence among the people of India and the world that a tyrannical communal regime and its unholy alliance with domestic and foreign corporates, and with imperialism itself, could be defeated. It was indeed a victory for sovereignty, for democracy, for secularism, and for the Constitution of India itself.

31. ROLE OF AIKS IN THE FARMERS' STRUGGLE

The All India Kisan Sabha (AIKS) has been an important constituent of the AIKSCC and the SKM ever since their inception. In this capacity, it played a major role in the collective decision making and implementation of the historic farmers' struggle. Whenever contentious issues arose, the AIKS always took a principled stand on them, in the direction of strengthening the unity of the SKM. This was generally appreciated by the other organizations.

DISTINCTIVE FEATURES OF AIKS CONTRIBUTION

Within the SKM, the AIKS took the initiative to strengthen worker-peasant unity, and the unity of farmers with other sections of the people. The SKM thus publicly supported the demand of the CTUs to repeal the four Labour Codes and a halt to the privatization drive of the public sector. Joint meetings of the SKM and the CTUs were held to coordinate nationwide actions. The SKM's national convention in August 2021 at the Singhu border invited leaders of the trade unions, agricultural workers, Dalit, Adivasi, women, youth and student organizations and adopted resolutions in support of their demands. This united approach helped make the Bharat Bandh of 27 September an unprecedented success.

While resolutely taking active part in all the SKM's joint nationwide calls, some independent actions were also organized. The most effective was the CITU-AIKS-AIAWU call for the nationwide struggle on the anniversary of 'Quit India Day', 9 August 2021. This 'Save India Day' mobilized lakhs of toilers all over the country. Another was the week-long padayatras organized by the AIKS and its fraternal organizations in Punjab, Haryana and Uttar Pradesh, culminating at the Delhi borders on Martyrs' Day, 23 March. The AIKS also organized several such independent actions during the year in several states.

The AIKS was the only peasant organization with a fair presence at all the six borders around Delhi. This AIKS mobilization came from the frontline states of Punjab, Haryana, Rajasthan, Uttar Pradesh and Madhya Pradesh.

The AIKS from various other states also took the lead in sending sizable contingents of peasants to the Delhi borders for several days each. They included Maharashtra, Kerala, Tamilnadu, Bihar, West Bengal, Gujarat, Telangana, Andhra Pradesh, Karnataka, Assam, Odisha, Chhattisgarh, Uttarakhand, Himachal Pradesh and Jammu & Kashmir.

Besides, all SKM struggle calls in the one year long struggle were well implemented in all the 23 states where the AIKS has its units, with a total mobilization of lakhs, putting it in the forefront among all SKM constituents.

Large Mahapanchayats under the SKM/AIKSCC banner, with good AIKS mobilization, were held in Kolkata, Mumbai, Agartala, Patna, Darbhanga, Samastipur, Bengaluru, Belgavi, Hyderabad, Visakhapatnam, Vijayawada, Ongole, Chennai, Thanjavur, Kanyakumari, Thiruvarur, Bhubaneswar, Ranchi, Thiruvananthapuram and all other district centres of Kerala, and hundreds of other places in the frontline states like Haryana, Punjab, Uttar Pradesh, Rajasthan, Madhya Pradesh and Uttarakhand. The AIKS participation in the SKM Kisan Mahapanchayats, especially in Muzaffarnagar, Lucknow and several other places, was impressive.

The frontline states and all other states of the AIKS did commendable work during this struggle. AIKS activists all over the country were, in fact, incessantly on the streets since 23 April 2020, when the first call for mass action was given, within a month of the declaration of the first lockdown on 24 March 2020. After the nationwide farmers' struggle began on 26 November 2020, the level of AIKS activity, of course, increased exponentially. Several struggles on local issues were taken up and linked to the national issues.

Despite the serious difficulties in the Covid pandemic, AIKS membership increased marginally. In 2019-20 it was 1,17,32,759 and in 2020-21 it was 1,17,41,513.

The AIKS Centre during this struggle published thousands of copies of pamphlets in both Hindi and English, and these were brought out in several national languages.

AIKS central journals *Kisan Sangharsh* (Hindi) and *Peasants' Struggle* (English), as well as several state journals, were published from time to time and sold very well.

Lakhs of AIKS flags and badges were brought out and they made an impressive impact.

THE AIKS LEADERSHIP

Among the AIKS leaders who camped at the Delhi borders braving heat, cold and rain, and were active in the frontline states were Major Singh Punnewal, Dharampal Singh Seal, Baljit Singh Grewal and Baldev Singh Latala from Punjab; Inderjit Singh, Surendra Singh, Phool Singh Sheokand, Sumit Dalal, Virender Singh Malik and Shraddhanand Solanki from Haryana; D P Singh, Chandrapal Singh, Mukut Singh, Bharat Singh and Digambar Singh from Uttar Pradesh; Amra Ram, Pema Ram, Chhagan Lal Choudhary, Sanjay Madhav and Pawan Duggal from Rajasthan; and Badal Saroj, Jaswinder Singh, Ashok Tiwari, Ramnarayan Kurariya, Akhilesh Yadav and Neena Sharma from Madhya Pradesh.

Apart from these leaders of the frontline states, thousands of leaders and activists of the AIKS, CITU, AIAWU, AIDWA, DYFI and SFI from all other states put in great efforts over the last one year to expand this struggle to their states in a big way.

The AIKS Centre during this year long struggle was

collectively manned by general secretary Hannan Mollah, myself as president, finance secretary P. Krishnaprasad and joint secretary Vijoo Krishnan. Joint secretaries N K Shukla, Badal Saroj and K.K. Ragesh were also at the Centre from time to time. The AIKS centre met regularly during this period, and also the extended centre comprising leading comrades from the frontline states.

All the comrades at the AIKS Centre regularly attended meetings in several states and participated in mass actions, including many large Kisan Mahapanchayats across the country.

The AIKS central office and all its multifarious tasks during this challenging period of struggle were efficiently handled by Sumit Ray, Manoj Kumar and Niloo Srivastava.

The 9-member coordination committee of the SKM included Hannan Mollah. However, because of his health, many meetings were attended by P. Krishnaprasad and myself in the last several months. Apart from the three of us, SKM general body meetings were regularly attended by Inderjit Singh, Major Singh Punnewal, Sumit, and at times by Amra Ram, Vijoo Krishnan, and some other leaders from Punjab and Haryana.

Hannan Mollah represented the AIKS in the 40-member group that had 11 rounds of talks with the central government till 22 January, when the government broke off talks.

I represented the AIKS in the 5-member committee of the SKM that was formed to negotiate the final agreement on pending issues with the central government.

After the victorious suspension of the struggle on 11 December, a meeting of all the leading AIKS activists of the frontline states of this struggle was held in Delhi on 21 December 2021. And the meeting of the All India Kisan Council (AIKC) of the AIKS was held in Hyderabad on 10-11 January 2022. These meetings discussed and decided upon a blueprint for future agitational, ideological and organizational work.

It was decided that paramount importance would be given to preserve and strengthen the unity of the SKM, while striving to enhance the independent strength and influence of the AIKS.

AIKS-CITU-AIAWU COORDINATION

A welcome feature was that the central leadership of the CITU, AIKS and AIAWU held several regular joint meetings in Delhi to plan out their joint strategy in the last one year. Two online countrywide public meetings by all three class organizations were held, the first on 8 May 2021 and the second on 24 June. Another online public meeting was held by the Save Democracy Forum on 26 June. It was addressed by Emergency detenus from several states.

Now this process of CITU-AIKS-AIAWU coordination is being systematically taken down to the states, with joint meetings of state office bearers of all three class organizations held in over 20 states, attended by their central office bearers. These prepared for the countrywide campaign from 25 July to 8 August, to culminate in the massive joint mass actions that took place on 'Save India Day', 9 August 2021. With these consistent efforts, the All India General Strike and Rural Hartal on 28-29 March 2022 were also made a grand success.

Special and commendable mention must be made of the large contributions to the AIKS Struggle Fund that were made during the course of the struggle by the working class, several unions affiliated to the CITU, many unions in the public sector and other well wishers.

AIDWA-DYFI-SFI also coordinated among themselves, and also with the AIKS-CITU-AIAWU, both at the Centre and in several states, and mobilized in thousands for the several actions in this year long farmers' struggle all over the country.

THE UNFINISHED STRUGGLE

The repeal of the three Farm Laws was indeed a historic

victory for the farmers and the people, and a humiliating defeat for the forces of corporate communalism.

However, several other key issues still remain. They include the legal guarantee of a remunerative MSP and procurement; sharp cuts in the rising prices of agricultural inputs; massive expansion towards a universal PDS with additional items; withdrawal of the Electricity Amendment Bill; freedom from indebtedness; a comprehensive crop insurance scheme; significant expansion of credit, irrigation and power facilities; a repeal of the four Labour Codes; halving the astronomical prices of diesel, petrol, cooking gas and other essential commodities; doubling the days of work and wages for agricultural workers under the MGNREGA; the starting of an Urban Employment Guarantee Scheme; guarantee of minimum wage of Rs 21,000 per month to all sections of unorganized workers; withdrawal of the New Education Policy; and most important, radical land reforms and a halt to the selling off of the country for a pittance to the corporates through the central government's privatization drive of the public sector.

With the inspiring impetus gained by the victory of this farmers' struggle, the people's struggle for the above demands, a policy change, and a regime change must and will go forth with even greater strength, confidence and determination!

One historic battle has been won. But the war remains.

We shall fight it! And we shall win that too!

POSTSCRIPT

THE ROOTS OF THE AGRARIAN CRISIS IN INDIA

The agrarian question continues to be the foremost national question before the people of India. Its resolution requires revolutionary change, including radical and thoroughgoing agrarian reforms that target abolition of landlordism, moneylender-merchant exploitation and caste and gender oppression in the countryside. The bankruptcy of the bourgeois-landlord rule in India is nowhere more evident than in its failure to address, much less solve, the agrarian question in a progressive, democratic way.

To advance towards its aim of an agrarian revolution, the All India Kisan Sabha (AIKS), which was formed at its foundation conference at Lucknow on 11 April 1936, led a series of momentous struggles in the 1940s. These struggles have been engraved in letters of gold in the annals of the peasant movement in India.

They include the struggles of Tebhaga in Bengal, Punnapra–Vayalar and North Malabar in Kerala, Gana Mukti Parishad in Tripura, Surma Valley in Assam, the revolt of the Warli Adivasis in Maharashtra, and crowned by the armed peasant uprising in Telangana.

All these struggles were directed against feudalism in all its forms. They demanded the abolition of the zamindari system and advocated radical land reforms. They were fought with the land question as their central agenda.

In the period after independence, it is no accident that only the Left-led state governments in Kerala, West Bengal and Tripura enacted legislation and carried out a programme of substantial land reforms and redistribution of land to the landless. The Jammu and Kashmir government under Shaikh Abdullah also carried out such land reforms.

THE STATE-SPONSORED PHASE OF CAPITALIST DEVELOPMENT

After independence, instead of abolishing landlordism and initiating radical land reforms, the Congress governments adopted policies to develop capitalism in agriculture without destroying the feudal base. Their aim was to transform semi-feudal landlords into capitalist landlords and develop a stratum of rich peasants. Land reforms were given the go by. Legislative measures to abolish statutory landlordism permitted the payment of huge compensation to landlords and allowed them to retain vast tracts of land. Provision for the right of resumption in tenancy laws led to the eviction of millions of tenants. Loopholes in land ceiling laws helped landlords keep large holdings intact.

P.C. Mahalanobis had estimated in the late 1950s that no less than 63 million acres of land in the country could be made available for redistribution. Not even a small fraction of this land was ever taken over or distributed to agricultural workers or poor peasants, except in Left-led states where, as mentioned above, a concerted effort was made to implement land reforms within the limitations of the state structure. A large number of the beneficiaries of these land reforms were peasants from the Scheduled Castes and Scheduled Tribes, who have traditionally been landless. Land concentration remained more or less unchanged in the rest of the country.

Capitalist development in Indian agriculture was not based on a resolute destruction of feudalism and older forms, but was superimposed on a swamp of pre-capitalist production relations and forms of social organization. This was a major factor in the continuance of caste and gender oppression. It also contributed in no small measure to the rise of communal and casteist forces.

Along with land concentration, government policies also ensured that irrigation and power facilities, subsidies to agricultural inputs, institutional credit facilities, agricultural implements, high-yielding seeds, fertilisers, pesticides, tube-wells, pump sets, vehicles, transport and other infrastructure facilities were cornered by landlords and rich peasants. It was these sections that became the influential support base of the bourgeois-landlord political parties in rural India.

Despite all these serious limitations, it was nevertheless true that the State-sponsored phase of capitalist development had certain positive features, which are now being negated in the neoliberal phase. For instance, in the earlier phase, governments made public investments for the expansion of irrigation, power, science and technology, research and development, transport, communications, storage facilities, and considerable progresss made in these areas. Investment in science and technology helped develop high yielding seeds and agricultural implements for increasing productivity and production. This led to the Green Revolution. Subsidies were provided for the purchase of agricultural inputs.

Measures were taken to protect the interests of producers by establishing a minimum support price and procurement mechanism in the case of certain crops. The public distribution system was set up with a degree of government subsidy. Efforts were made to provide institutional credit facilities to farmers, especially after the nationalization of banks. Priority was given to increasing food grain production and attaining food grain self-sufficiency. Restrictions were put on the import and export of agricultural commodities in order to protect the domestic market.

Although the lion's share of the benefits of these measures was appropriated by the rural rich, these steps nevertheless helped the agrarian sector as a whole to achieve certain levels of growth and development.

Analysing the Green Revolution, former AIKS President S.R. Pillai wrote, 'The technology of the Green Revolution was introduced by the ruling classes with three clear-cut objectives: one, the fear of agrarian revolution; second, to develop capitalist relations in agriculture; third, to serve two types of interests, those of the Indian capitalists and of the multinational agri-business firms producing fertilisers, pesticides, weedicides and agricultural machineries. The technology of the Green Revolution was meant to increase productivity and production in agriculture making use of high-yielding seed varieties and modern inputs. It was claimed that once this technology was successfully implemented, India would not have to look back and an era of never ending agricultural prosperity would ensue. It soon became clear that this recipe for curing all agricultural ills was not meant for all the peasants and all the regions. It was based on a 'selective strategy' of distributing the seeds, fertilisers, pesticides, tillers, tractors only to those areas which have developed institutional infrastructure facilitated by irrigation, credit and other factors. This helped to increase productivity and production, but along with that, two types of inequalities also developed – the inequality between regions and the inequality between peasants.'

In the light of experience, the 23rd national conference of the AIKS held at Varanasi in 1979 made an important departure. It stated as follows: 'Taking note of these structural changes and their multifarious consequences, we have to come to the conclusion that the slogan of complete abolition of landlordism and distribution of land to the landless and the land-poor continues to be the central slogan of the agrarian revolution, a slogan which we have to continue to propagate. But it is a slogan on which we cannot go into action today in most parts of the country. While continuing to propagate this as the central slogan, while continuing struggles for surplus land, benami lands, waste lands etc, the Kisan Sabha will have to take up for immediate action such issues as the question of wages of agricultural workers, house-sites, rent-reduction, 75 per cent of the produce to the sharecroppers, evictions, abolition or scaling down of rural indebtedness, remunerative price for agricultural produce, cheap credit, reduction of tax burdens and heavy levies like water charges, electricity rates etc, landlord goonda attacks with the connivance or direct help of the police, the social oppression of dalits, corruption in administration etc. These are the issues which affect all sections of the peasantry – poor, middle, rich – and they can all be drawn into the movement on them. All these currents have to be brought together to build the maximum unity of the peasantry centering around the agricultural workers and poor peasants to isolate the small stratum of landlords.'

This understanding at the Varanasi conference of the AIKS was further concretized in the 'Statement of Policy' adopted in the Golden Jubilee conference of the AIKS at Patna in 1986.

THE NEO-LIBERAL PHASE OF CAPITALIST DEVELOPMENT

Neo-liberal policies, in agriculture in particular, were begun by the Congress central government in 1991. They witnessed a reactionary change in the policies of the State under imperialist pressure. This phase is based on the retreat of the State from economic affairs and its surrender to the capitalist market.

Two major factors led to the neoliberal phase of capitalist development. One was that the monopoly capitalists, landlords and other richer sections that had benefited and gained strength and assets during the first phase expected to achieve even more benefits under the neoliberal regime. Besides, the State-sponsored phase had reached an impasse, resulting in a crisis by the late 1980s.

The other factor was the growing attempt of the imperialist countries to dominate the world after the collapse of socialism in the Soviet Union and East Europe from 1989 to 1991. The imperislist countries and multinational corporations began using international financial institutions like the International Monetary

Fund (IMF), World Bank (WB), and after 1994 the World Trade Organization (WTO), to pressurize other countries, especially in the developing world, to accept the neoliberal regime.

The neoliberal policies in agriculture have the following basic components:

1. Reversal of land reforms and and dilution of land ceiling laws to enable the sale or lease of vast tracts of land to Indian big business and foreign multinationals.
2. Slashing of government subsidies on seeds, fertilisers, irrigation, electricity and other inputs leading to a massive rise in the cost of agricultural inputs and a consequent sharp rise in the cost of production.
3. Removal of quantitative restrictions on agricultural imports and reduction of import duties, leading to a flood of heavily subsidized foreign agricultural goods with a resultant crash in the prices of domestic agricultural products. Free Trade Agreements (FTAs) have the same impact.
4. Sharp cuts in public investment in agriculture, irrigation, power, rural development, science and technology, research and development, other infrastructural facilities, and overall reduction in allocation for the agricultural sector.
5. Privatization of the vital sectors of electricity and irrigation, resulting in high costs of both and also in the creation of water monopolies.
6. A severe crunch in institutional credit to peasants and agricultural workers, due to the policy direction of siphoning off of large chunks of credit to the corporates, increasing the dependence of the peasantry on usurious private money-lenders.
7. Drastic curtailment of food subsidies and launching a targeted public distribution system instead of the earlier

universal one, endangering food security for the poor.

8. Withdrawal of the government from domestic market intervention measures like the minimum support price mechanism and the procurement system of crops.
9. A policy thrust towards export-oriented agriculture, changing the cropping pattern away from food crops towards cash crops and giving up priority for food grain production.
10. Growing mechanization of agricultural operations and sharp reduction in the employment and real wages of agricultural workers.
11. Watering down of schemes of rural employment, poverty alleviation, public education, public health, housing and other social welfare measures, accompanied by privatization of education and health services.
12. The invasion of rapacious multinational corporations and domestic corporates in all agricultural sectors to the detriment of the peasantry and the consumers; and the new patent regime, which surrenders India's independence for its biological resources and hijacks our traditional knowledge of seeds and plants.

The 27th national conference of the AIKS held at Hisar in 1992 was the first after the beginning of the neoliberal policies. It tore apart the neoliberal policies and warned,

> The present policies of the Union government will have a serious adverse impact on the peasantry. This will speed up pauperization of the poor, the small and middle peasants. The number of unemployed youth, both in the urban and the rural sides will again rise to unprecedented heights.

The seminal address of the then AIKS president Harkishan Singh Surjeet at this conference elaborated on these and other aspects further. Significantly, the AIKS made this assessment of the neoliberal policies within a year, when almost all other peasant organizations were supporting the new economic and agricultural policies. The warnings of the Hisar conference were more than vindicated by agrarian developments over the last 30 years.

The impact of more than three decades of neoliberal policies on Indian agriculture has been disastrous. Over four lakh farmers have been forced to die by suicide due to indebtedness in the 25 years from 1995 to 2020. Lakhs of children in the tribal and dalit areas of the country have died of starvation and malnutrition. Poverty and hunger are spreading to newer sections and areas. Unemployment is sky-rocketing. Migration is growing rapidly.

TWO BASIC RURAL CONTRADICTIONS

'The Alternative Agricultural Policy' document adopted by the AIKS and the All India Agricultural Workers Union (AIAWU) in December 2003 broadly divided the post-independence period of capitalist development in agriculture into two phases as explained above – the state-sponsored phase from 1947 to 1990 and the neoliberal phase from 1991 onwards. In the light of this, it outlined the two main rural contradictions as follows:

> From the above analysis, it is clear that the present situation in Indian agriculture is characterized by two important contradictions. The first is the sharp division between the rural rich, comprising landlords, big capitalist farmers, large traders, money-lenders and their allies on the one hand and the mass of the peasantry, comprising agricultural workers, poor and middle peasants and rural artisans on the other. The second is the growing opposition to imperialist-driven neoliberal policies of the government, not only from the mass of the peasantry but also from sections of the rural rich.

In the liberalization phase, the primitive accumulation of capital is ruining Indian agriculture and is assaulting the Indian peasantry. Land reforms have acquired a reverse meaning. It is no longer land to the tiller, but land to the corporates. This is glaringly seen in the policy of the Special Economic Zones, the various proposed industrial corridors and in the attempt by the Modi-led BJP government at the very beginning of its tenure to ram through the hated Land Acquisition Amendment Ordinance. This attempt was foiled through a combination of united peasant struggles on the ground and concerted opposition in the upper house in Parliament.

Profit maximization is being sought by squeezing the peasantry through neoliberal agricultural policies. These policies are fuelling the catastrophic phenomenon of lakhs of deaths by suicide of debt-ridden peasants in the last three decades. First, the slashing of subsidies and a free hand to rapacious MNCs and domestic corporates in the production of agricultural inputs lead to a massive increase in the cost of production. Second, the consistent refusal to give remunerative prices for agricultural produce under the pressure of foreign finance capital, a glut in agricultural imports that further ruin the peasantry, a slew of free trade agreements, a crunch in the formal agricultural credit, and siphoning it away to the corporates, thus leading to increased dependence of farmers on usurious private moneylenders. And third, a series of natural calamities like drought, floods, hailstorms as well as attacks by pests and by wild animals, a bogus crop insurance scheme designed to benefit not farmers but insurance companies, savage cuts in public investment for irrigation and power. These are some of the main aspects of the neoliberal attacks on agriculture that are responsible for rising peasant indebtedness, alarming peasant deaths by suicide, and land alienation.

These aspects have to be fought tooth and nail by the peasant movement.

WORST CULPRIT: BJP-RSS' MODI REGIME

The present BJP-RSS central government has been the worst culprit in intensifying neoliberal policies in agriculture, industry and all other sectors under imperialist dictates. BJP-led state governments have naturally followed suit.

The General Secretary's Report presented by Hannan Mollah to the 34th National Conference of the AIKS held at Hisar, Haryana from 3-6 October 2017 analysed in detail the agrarian changes in the last 25 years of liberalization in the section titled 'Changes in Agrarian Relations and Class Differentiation'. It then outlined the disastrous agrarian scenario under the current BJP-RSS regime which has betrayed every single promise of 'Achche Din' made to farmers by the BJP election manifesto of 2014. We shall here just enumerate some of the major aspects and results of BJP-RSS rule that have been analysed in that report. These are:

- Intensified agrarian crisis and unabated peasant suicides;
- Rapid increase in landlessness and land inequality;
- Unprecedented land grab and dispossession of the peasantry;
- Attack on forest rights and loot of resources;
- Financial liberalization and indebtedness;
- Enamour for free trade and economic liberalism;
- Demonetization and GST attack on the peasantry;
- Corporatization of agriculture;
- Doubling farmers' woes instead of incomes;
- Incessant fall in agricultural prices;
- Acute human tragedy amidst drought, floods and government apathy;
- Attack on MGNREGA and rural employment;
- Increased vulnerability of women in agriculture;
- Notification restricting cattle trade;

- Menace of wild animals and stray cattle;
- Climate change and compromise at the Paris summit;
- Grave authoritarian and communal attacks on democracy and secularism.

On top of all this came the three anti-farmer, anti-people and pro-corporate Farm Laws, which the Modi regime was forced to repeal as a result of the farmers' struggle.

But the neoliberal policy direction of this regime will not change. Much greater dangers lie ahead if this regime is not defeated. The farmers' movement will have to put up even stiffer and more united resistance, just as it did last year.

And most important, it will also have to politically and ideologically combat and defeat the menacing scourge of communalism, casteism and authoritarianism.

APPENDIX 1

TIMELINE OF THE FARMERS' STRUGGLE

The major milestones in the farmers' struggle in India of 2020-21 were as follows:

November 25-26, 2020 – Farmers' struggle begins with lakhs of farmers from Punjab and Haryana braving intense repression by the BJP-JJP Haryana state government and the central government. 26 November is also the day of the massive All India Strike against the four Labour Codes by the working class. The struggle thus begins on the significant note of worker-peasant unity. 26 November is also Constitution Day, the day the Constitution of India was adopted by the Constituent Assembly in 1949.

December 8 – Unprecedented first Bharat Bandh in support of the farmers' struggle; call given for boycott of Ambani and Adani products and services.

December – Toll plazas freed in Punjab, Haryana and later in parts of Rajasthan.

December 31 – LDF government tables resolution for repeal of three Farm Laws in Kerala state assembly, becoming the first assembly in India to unanimously adopt it.

January 12, 2021 – Supreme Court stays implementation of the three Farm Laws for one and a half year, but appoints four-member pro-government committee, of whom one member immediately resigns; committee's reactionary report recently made public.

January 18 – Mahila Kisan Day observed at Delhi borders and all over the country.

January 22 – BJP government breaks off talks with the SKM after 11 rounds.

January 23-26 – Massive Kisan Mahapadavs and rallies in various state capitals mobilize lakhs of peasants and workers in several states across India.

January 26 – Huge peaceful one lakh strong tractor rally by lakhs of farmers on Republic Day; it is disrupted with the Red Fort incident by the BJP government's chosen agent provocateurs; 'Godi' media goes on rampage against the farmers' struggle.

January 27-29 – Farmers at Delhi borders bravely fight back intense state repression.

January 29 – MPs of opposition parties boycott President's Address in Parliament in support of the valiant farmers' struggle.

January 30 – Mahatma Gandhi's Martyrdom Anniversary observed countrywide, stressing his tenets of truth and non-violence, which guide the farmers' struggle.

February 6 – Countrywide Road Blocks at 3000 centres against government repression.

February 18 – Militant Rail Roko struggle at 600 centres across the country.

February to April – Hundreds of massive Kisan Mazdoor Mahapanchayats across the country, which mobilize lakhs of peasants and workers against the Modi regime.

March 6 – Farmers' struggle completes 100 days, KMP highway blocked, countrywide demonstrations of support.

March 8 – International Women's Day widely observed in solidarity.

March 15 – SKM supports Anti Privatization Day call by Central Trade Unions.

March 18-23 – AIKS and its fraternal organizations conduct series of impressive padayatras from Punjab, Haryana and Uttar Pradesh and bring them to Delhi borders.

March 23 – Martyrdom Anniversary of Bhagat Singh, Rajguru and Sukhdev observed countrywide as Youth Kisan Day.

March 26 – Second Bharat Bandh in support of the farmers in struggle to coincide with the completion of four months of the struggle.

April 10-11 – KMP Highway blocked for 24 hours.

April 14 – Countrywide observance of Birth Anniversary of Dr B R Ambedkar as 'Save Constitution Day'.

April – Farmers foil Covid-related 'Operation Clean' plan of government to clear Delhi borders through 'Operation Shakti', despite the deadly second Covid wave.

April-May – Farmers help Covid patients in distress in Delhi during deadly second wave.

May 2 – Stinging defeat of BJP and its allies in the state assembly elections in Kerala, Tamilnadu and West Bengal widely celebrated all over the country.

May 10 – Beginning of First War of Indian Independence of 1857 observed.

May 26 – Six months of the farmers' struggle and seven years of the Modi government observed as Black Flag Day with burning of effigies of the Modi regime countrywide.

June 5 – Protests to mark one year of the three Farm Ordinances.

June 6 – Public meetings to pay homage to the six Mandsaur martyrs of 2017, killed in police firing by the BJP state government of Madhya Pradesh.

June 9 – Martyrdom Anniversary observed of legendary tribal freedom fighter of Jharkhand, Birsa Munda, who died in a British jail in 1900.

June 18 – Martyrdom Anniversary observed of Rani Laxmibai of Jhansi, killed in 1858 during the First War of Indian Independence.

June 26 – Renowned American Left intellectual Noam Chomsky supports the farmers' struggle in India, calls it 'a beacon of light in dark times for the entire world'.

June 26 – Completion of seven months of the farmers' struggle and 46 years after the imposition of the Emergency; call to fight undeclared Emergency of the Modi regime widely observed all over the country.

June 30 – Anniversary of the tribal peasants' Santhal Rebellion of 1855 against the British, observed as 'Hul Kranti Divas'.

July 8 – Nationwide protests against the massive price hikes of diesel, petrol and gas.

July 17 – People's Whips issued to MPs to fight for farmers in Parliament session.

July 22 to August 9 – Hundreds of farmers hold Kisan Parliament at Jantar Mantar daily during Parliament's monsoon session; July 26 and August 9 see women farmers' sessions; Kisan Parliament adopts several resolutions on farmers' issues, and concludes by adopting a No Confidence Motion against the Modi government.

July 26 – 'Mission Uttar Pradesh' and 'Mission Uttarakhand' to defeat the BJP governments in these states declared at SKM press conference in Lucknow.

August 9 – Lakhs of peasants, workers and other sections in India led by AIKS, CITU, AIAWU, AIDWA, DYFI, SFI hit the streets to mark 'Save India Day'.

August 15 – Lakhs join Tiranga Rallies on Independence Day all over the country to mark it as 'Kisan Mazdoor Azaadi Sangram Divas'.

August 20 – 19 opposition parties in India release a joint statement on 11 burning demands, supporting key demands of the farmers' and workers' struggle.

August 24 – Sugarcane farmers of Punjab gain victory with a price of Rs 360 per quintal, a Rs 50 increase, after five days of Rail Roko and Rasta Roko.

August 26-27 – SKM National Convention at Singhu border mobilizes over 2000 people, including national leaders of trade unions, agricultural workers, dalits, adivasis, women, youth and students; Gives call for Bharat Bandh on September 27.

August 28 – Brutal repression by police of Haryana BJP-JJP regime at Karnal claims one martyr; intense struggle by SKM begins against repression.

September 5 – Kisan Mazdoor Mahapanchayat of 10 lakhs at Muzaffarnagar, UP, cutting across religion, caste, state and language. Mission Uttar Pradesh inaugurated.

September 7-11 – Karnal siege in Haryana against repression leads to victory.

September 25 – Two Muslim peasants, one of them a 12 year-old boy, in Darrang, Assam, killed in police firing ordered by the BJP state regime; condemnation all over.

September 27 – Third Bharat Bandh in the farmers' struggle gets unprecedented response from crores of farmers, workers and the people all over the country.

September 28 – Shaheed Bhagat Singh Birth Anniversary widely observed in India.

October 2 – Mahatma Gandhi Birth Anniversary widely observed all over the country.

October 3 – Stunning massacre of mowing down of four farmers and a journalist at Lakhimpur Kheri in Uttar Pradesh by convoy of cars belonging to BJP Union Minister of State for Home Ajay Mishra Teni, driven by his son Ashish Mishra and other BJP goons.

October 4/5 – SKM gives countrywide protest call to denounce this massacre.

October 11 – Massive Maharashtra Bandh called by the ruling Maha Vikas Aghadi, and supported by all Left and anti-BJP forces, to condemn the Lakhimpur Kheri massacre.

October 11 – Birth Anniversary of Jayaprakash Narayan widely observed.

October 12 – Huge condolence meeting to mark Antim Ardaas of farmer martyrs at Lakhimpur Kheri; large protest meetings and candle light vigils across the country; Shaheed Kalash Yatras begin in several states with large farmers' gatherings.

October 15 – To mark Dussehra, effigies of BJP leaders Modi, Shah, Yogi, Mishra, Tomar and Khattar burnt by lakhs of people at thousands of places in India to denounce the Lakhimpur Kheri massacre and to demand the dismissal and arrest of Ajay Mishra.

October 15 – Unfortunate incident of the murder of a Dalit Sikh agricultural worker by other Dalit Sikhs owing allegiance to a Nihang sect at Singhu border, over the alleged desecration of a religious text; SKM condemns the incident and alleges a BJP conspiracy to defame the farmers' struggle; this conspiracy is confirmed within four days with the publication of a photograph and news of Nihang chief Baba Aman Singh meeting BJP agriculture minister Narendra Singh Tomar, and other shady characters.

October 16 – India slips further in World Hunger Index, from 94th place out of 107 countries, to 101st place out of 116 countries.

October 18 – Countrywide Rail Roko to demand dismissal and arrest of Ajay Mishra.

October 26 – 11 months of farmers' struggle, countrywide demonstrations to demand dismissal and arrest of Ajay Mishra.

November 2 – BJP defeated in by-elections in Himachal, Haryana and Rajasthan.

November 11 – National Trade Union Convention in Delhi gives call for two day All India General Strike against Modi regime's policies on March 28-29, 2022.

November 15 – Birth Anniversary of Adivasi freedom fighter Birsa

Munda observed.

November 16 – Martyrdom Anniversary of Ghadar Party warriors Kartar Singh Sarabha and Vishnu Ganesh Pingle, and of Dalit woman fighter of the 1857 War, Veerangana Uda Devi Pasi, observed.

November 19 – On Guru Nanak Jayanti, Narendra Modi finally announces in an address to the nation that the three hated Farm Laws would be repealed.

November 19-21 – Spontaneous celebrations by farmers and workers all over the country at the repeal declaration.

November 21 – SKM sends an open letter to the Prime Minister listing pending demands.

November 22 – SKM holds massive Mahapanchayat at Lucknow, capital of UP.

November 25 – SKM holds large Mahadharna at Hyderabad, capital of Telangana.

November 26 – Completion of one year of the farmers' struggle; massive mobilizations at Delhi borders and in the states celebrate victory, vow to fight for pending demands.

November 28 – SKM holds massive Mahapanchayat at Mumbai, capital of Maharashtra.

November 29 – Both Houses of Parliament repeal the three black Farm Laws.

December 2 – Presidential assent to the repeal of the three black Farm Laws.

December 4 – SKM appoints 5-member committee to negotiate the pending demands with the central government.

December 6 – Death Anniversary of Dr B R Ambedkar widely observed.

December 7 – SKM meeting rejects first draft of letter from central government, insists on important changes.

December 8 – SKM's 5-member committee meets at AIKS office in Delhi; SKM meeting accepts revised second draft of letter from central government, which makes most of the changes insisted upon by SKM.

December 9 – Central government's Agriculture Secretary sends official letter to SKM conceding most demands; massive SKM meeting accepts it, calls for suspension of struggle from December 11, which will be observed as Victory Day all over the country.

December 11 – Victory Day massively celebrated all across India; tens of thousands of farmers start returning home from all the Delhi borders after over one year.

Social boycott of, and hundreds of peaceful black flag demonstrations against, BJP-JJP leaders in Haryana and BJP leaders in Punjab, Uttar Pradesh, Uttarakhand, Rajasthan, Madhya Pradesh, etc., continued unabated for the last several months.

Lastly, one important and welcome feature was the international solidarity that this farmers' struggle received worldwide; there were solidarity rallies by the Indian diaspora and other citizens in the UK, USA, Canada, France, Australia, New Zealand, and other countries of Europe and elsewhere. Many of them were led by the Left.

APPENDIX 2

MANIFESTO OF INDIAN FARMERS

(Adopted by an assembly representing the farmers of India at the Kisan Mukti March organized by the All India Kisan Sangharsh Coordination Committee, Delhi, 30 November 2018)

WE, THE FARMERS OF INDIA,

The producers of primary agricultural commodities;

Including Women, Dalit, Nomadic and Adivasi farmers;

Landowners, Tenants, Sharecroppers, Agricultural Labourers and Plantation Workers;

Fishworkers, Milk Producers, Poultry Farmers, Livestock Rearers, Pastoralists, and Collectors of Minor Forest Produce; and,

Everyone engaged in crop cultivation, shifting cultivation, apiculture, sericulture, vermiculture, and agro-forestry;

CONVINCED THAT

Wellbeing of farmers is not just about economic survival of a majority of Indian households, it is about retaining our national dignity and our civilizational heritage;

Farmers are not just a residue from our past; farmers, agriculture and village community are integral to the future of India and the world; and,

The demands of the farmers' movements are fully consistent with our Constitutional vision, Fundamental Rights and Directive Principles of State Policy;

RECOGNISING OUR RESPONSIBILITY

As honest hard workers who face numerous odds;

As bearers of historical knowledge, skills and culture;

As agents of food safety, security and sovereignty; and

As guardians of biodiversity and ecological sustainability;

RECALLING THE PRINCIPLES OF

Economic viability;

Ecological sustainability; and

Equality with social and economic justice;

YET ALARMED AT

Economic, ecological, social and existential crisis of Indian agriculture;

Ecological degradation and destruction affecting farmers and their livelihoods;

Unprecedented increase in diversion and destruction of agricultural land, privatization of water, forced displacement, deprivation and migration affecting security of food and livelihood;

Persistent state of neglect of agriculture and discrimination against farming communities;

Increasing vulnerability of farmers to extortion by the village powerful and government officials;

Deepening penetration of large, predatory and profiteering corporations that are already in control of significant sectors of Indian agriculture;

Spate of farmers' suicides across the country and unbearable burden of indebtedness;

Alarming deaths of adivasi and dalit children due to hunger and malnutrition;

Widening disparities between farmers and other sectors in our society; and,

Growing attack of the governments on the farmers' struggles;

SOLEMNLY AFFIRM OUR CONSTITUTIONAL RIGHT TO

Life and dignified livelihood;

Social security and protection against natural and other calamities;

Land, water, forest and all natural resources including common property resources;

Diversity in seeds, food systems and sustainable technological choices; and,

Freedom of expression, organization, representation and struggle through constitutional means for realization of our demands and shaping our future;

THEREFORE, CALL UPON THE PARLIAMENT OF INDIA TO IMMEDIATELY

Hold a Special Session to address the agrarian crisis by passing and enacting the two Kisan Mukti Bills that are of, by and for the farmers of India, namely,

1. The Farmers' Freedom from Indebtedness Bill, 2018; and
2. The Farmers' Right to Guaranteed Remunerative Minimum Support Prices for Agricultural Commodities Bill, 2018.

AND ALSO DEMAND THAT THE GOVERNMENT OF INDIA MUST

1. Increase the number of guaranteed employment days under MGNREGA to 200 days per family, and ensure wage payment within the period guaranteed by statute and at par with legal minimum wages for unskilled farm labour;
2. Reduce the cost of inputs for farmers either by regulating industry price or offering subsidy directly to farmers;
3. Provide comprehensive social security for all farm households including pension at least Rs. 5,000 per month per farmer above the age of 60;
4. Universalize the benefits of the Public Distribution System including cereals and nutri-cereals, pulses, sugar and oils without linking it to Aadhar or biometric identification and without shifting to direct cash transfer;
5. Address the menace of stray animals by removing all legal and vigilante-imposed restrictions on cattle trade, compensating farmers for destruction of crops by wild and stray animals and supporting animal shelters;
6. Stop land acquisition or land pooling without informed consent of the farmers; no acquisition or diversion of agricultural land for commercial land development or for creation of land banks; prevent the bypassing or dilution of The Right to Fair Compensation and

Transparency in Land Acquisition, Rehabilitation and Resettlement Act, 2013 at the central and state level; and evolve land use and agricultural land protection policy;

7. Mandate the sugar mills to pay interest at 15% p.a. if cane dues are not paid to the cane-growers within 14 days of the delivery of cane; FRP of cane to be fixed by linking it to 9.5% recovery of sugar;

8. Withdraw pesticides that have been banned elsewhere and not approve GM seeds without a comprehensive needs, alternatives and impact assessment;

9. Disallow Foreign Direct Investment in agriculture and food processing, and remove agriculture from Free Trade Agreements, including the proposed Regional Comprehensive Economic Partnership (RCEP);

10. Require identification and registration of all real cultivators including tenant farmers, sharecroppers, women farmers, lessee cultivators and rural workers etc. for purposes of accessing benefits of all government schemes; and

11. Stop uprooting adivasi farmers in the name of afforestation, ensure strict implementation without dilution of Panchayat (Extension to Scheduled Areas) Act and Forests Rights Act, 2006;

AND, FURTHER, URGE THE GOVERNMENT TO EVOLVE POLICIES TO

12. Provide land and livelihood rights to the landless, including agricultural and homestead land, water for fishing, mining of minor minerals etc;

13. Ensure timely, effective and adequate compensation for crop loss due to natural disasters; implement a comprehensive crop insurance scheme that benefits farmers and not just insurance companies and that covers all types of risks for all crops and for all farmers, with an individual farm as the unit of damage assessment; reverse anti-farmer changes in the Manual for Drought Management;

14. Build assured protective irrigation through sustainable means for farmers, especially in the rain-fed areas;

15. Ensure remunerative guaranteed prices for milk and its procurement for dairies and to supplement nutritional security through Mid Day Meal Scheme and Integrated Child Development Scheme etc;

16. Waive off all outstanding agricultural loans of farmers from suicide-affected families and provide special opportunities to children of such families;

17. Protect the farmers from corporate plunder in the name of contract farming by reviewing the Contract Farming Act 2018;

18. Promote procurement, processing and marketing under Farmer Producer Organizations and Peasant Cooperatives instead of corporatization of agriculture and takeover by MNCs; and

19. Promote an agro-ecology paradigm that is based on suitable cropping patterns and local seed diversity revival, so as to build economically viable, ecologically sustainable, autonomous and climate resilient agriculture.